God Took My Hand

God Took My Hand

Deacon Kevin R. Carges

authorHOUSE®

AuthorHouse™ LLC
1663 Liberty Drive
Bloomington, IN 47403
www.authorhouse.com
Phone: 1-800-839-8640

Published by AuthorHouse   08/01/2013

ISBN: 978-1-4918-0154-3 (sc)
ISBN: 978-1-4918-0127-7 (e)

Library of Congress Control Number: 2013913533

Any people depicted in stock imagery provided by Thinkstock are models, and such images are being used for illustrative purposes only.
Certain stock imagery © Thinkstock.

This book is printed on acid-free paper.

Because of the dynamic nature of the Internet, any web addresses or links contained in this book may have changed since publication and may no longer be valid. The views expressed in this work are solely those of the author and do not necessarily reflect the views of the publisher, and the publisher hereby disclaims any responsibility for them.

Jeremiah 1:4-9

The word of the Lord came to me, saying, "Before I formed you in the womb I knew you, Before you were born I set you apart;

I appointed you as a prophet to the nations."

"Ah, Sovereign Lord," I said, "I do not know how to speak; I am only a child."

But the Lord said to me, "Do not say, I am only a child. You must go to everyone I send you to and say whatever I command you. Do not be afraid of them, for I am with you and will rescue you," declares the Lord.

Then the Lord reached out his hand and touched my mouth and said to me, "Now, I have put my words in your mouth.

FOREWORD BY ROD CHRISTIAN

I Am Here For You, I Am Here With You"

Tourists love Jamaica for its sandy beaches and resorts. Kevin Carges loves Jamaica for its poor and destitute.

He was a changed man in February 2006 after returning from a mission trip to one of the poorest countries in the Western Hemisphere.

"I had seen poverty in other countries on television and had also read about it, so I thought I was aware," he says. "I thought I understood but after my time in Jamaica all I really knew was that I was a changed person. I came back devastated by what I had just experienced. I shed tears every day for weeks trying to comprehend what I had just taken in."

Kevin's transformation was total and complete and readily apparent even years later. He works tirelessly to rally others to support the country with financial donations and others forms of support. He founded Eight 4 Third World Hope, a non-profit agency whose mission is to raise funds for needed projects in Jamaica, such as schools and restroom facilities. The group works closely with Food for the Poor, the largest international relief agency in the U.S. Food for the Poor staff members in Jamaica identify potential funding projects for Eight 4 Third World Hope and set up mission trips for group members.

Ali Escalante of Food for the Poor saw firsthand Kevin's transformation after his trip to Jamaica.

"I know his first trip touched him deeply. Kevin's heart was not only touched by the poor, but broken by the poor," she says. "He has a deep, genuine concern for them. He has complete love for the less fortunate. He is a man of great faith and compassion."

As a deacon in the Catholic Church and the owner of a small business, as well as a family to provide for, it would have been easy for Kevin to given token attention to the plight of Jamaicans after returning from his first trip. Instead, he plunged in. He started his own website, called "Deacon Kevin's Circle of Friends," which, together with speaking engagements, raised over $10,000 in two years. He realized he needed help to make a greater impact.

The turning point was St. John Fisher College's 25th Alumni Reunion in 2009.

"As I looked around the room, I could see so many gifts and abilities that could be put to use. I knew these people so well. They were and are my friends. Knowing what kind of people they were, I knew they would respond when I asked them to help."

Thus was born Eight 4 Third World Hope . . . Kevin, six friends and former classmates, and the eighth member Christ, guiding the group's mission to serve. Kevin's personal crusade was about to change dramatically.

Four months after the group first met, they raised more than $10,000 with their first fundraising event, doubling the amount Kevin had raised on his own over two years. Three months later, Matt Shue secured a $10,000 grant from a foundation in Colorado. Two months after that, the group raised another $7,000 with another fundraising event at St. John Fisher, for a total of $27,000 in nine months. This was the goal they had set in their first meeting—$27,000 for a new elementary school for the students of Concord, Jamaica, a remote and mountainous area in the middle of the country.

Clearly, larger forces were at work.

"All it takes is a small, committed group to affect deep change," says Escalante. "Jesus only had twelve disciples. Look at what this group has already accomplished—great deeds, mighty deeds. God is working miracles through them. It was nothing short of a miracle for these communities to get a new school or an actual restroom facility. The principal of the school said so herself. You could see that she meant it when she gave the prayer on the day of the dedication."

"Eight 4 Third World Hope is one of the most genuine and dedicated groups I've had the privilege to work with. And it's the first alumni group that I've heard of that is doing work like this."

The second project was identified with help from Food for the Poor when Kevin and his daughter (and future board member) Allison visited Jamaica in January 2011. The Bensonton School, a secondary school, is located about 20 minutes from Concord. The students were using pit latrines, which presented several sanitary and psychological challenges for the students who had to use them. The school had never had restrooms until Eight 4 Third World Hope funded then with $11,000, raised largely from the group's first Wine & Cheese Reception at St. John Fisher College a few months earlier.

With so much momentum established so quickly, the group voted unanimously in the summer of 2011 to become a non-profit 501 c3 agency, so that it could raise funds from more diverse sources. The group received its charter a few months later.

In January 2012, a few of the group's members visited Jamaica with Escalante and other Food for the Poor staff. They attended the dedication of the new Sacred Heart School they had funded, as well as the dedication of the Bensonton school restroom facilities. They reviewed potential upcoming projects. They toured Food for the Poor's Jamaican operation center. Escalante was with the group throughout that week but none of the above left the deepest impression on her.

"The trip with Eight 4 Third World Hope inspired me, to see their genuine compassion for others. There was for me a palpable sense of selflessness on their part and such a strong concern for the poor."

"What was so beautiful was how they all got down on their knees to the level of the children and those in wheelchairs. They gave them a sense of I am here for you, I am here with you. I am a child of God too; I am your equal. I think that really came through."

"It may have been a different country and they may have been a different color, but it didn't matter. There was no hesitation to hug. They got a sense of how much they were valued and of God's love for them. It was very genuine compassion in action."

The group reflects Kevin's many virtues—humility, selflessness and treating others as brothers and sisters.

"It's easy to underestimate how mighty Kevin is," said Escalante. "He's a humble person but look at the support he's been able to mobilize. He empties himself so that others can be lifted up."

"It takes courage to ask for help, but each person who sees and hears the group's stories can share those with their family and friends. It's a ripple effect. The mustard seed in Kevin will continue to grow. That's the beauty of this."

As of summer 2012, almost $47,000 had been raised for the group's third and most ambitious project to date—a new school for the community of McCook's Pen. The current school is a school in name only. It is a shack by American standards, with a tin roof, decrepit walls, a tiny kitchen and an unsafe restroom. The name of the school is written in chalk on one of the outside walls. It is off an unmarked dirt road next to a graveyard and a few abandoned vehicles.

Kevin and the group are thrilled with what the group's donors will be providing these children—a new, modern school that reflects the special commitment of its principal, teacher and families. It is scheduled to open in 2013.

"I am seeing miracles happen," says Kevin. "We are changing lives and making a difference."

"Sometimes words are not enough, but that and some pictures are all I have. It saddens me that that I haven't been able to find the words to tell anyone how I truly feel inside."

— Kevin Carges

SO IT BEGINS

It is May 21, 2005 and I have just been ordained a Deacon in the Roman Catholic Church by Bishop Matthew Clark. I'm filled with so many emotions; joy, accomplishment, humbled beyond words that God has called me to this special ministry, but perhaps "lost" might be the best word. You see, I never wanted this. I didn't want to be a Deacon, I fought it all the way, tried to get out but couldn't. Sounds strange doesn't it? But God had plans for me, just like all of us, and I had to put my trust in Him as I learned and still continue to learn every day.

All along the way I didn't see it coming, I had no idea or even a thought about where I would end up, but here I am, and now I am writing a book about it, something else I never dreamed I would do. It is not meant to be about me, although you the reader will be reading my words and sharing my emotions. This book is intended to tell the stories of those I met along this journey of mine these past twelve years. It is also a story of how God prepared me for this life of serving others, those with no voice in particular. This book is intended to be their voice and story.

I think that it is only fair that you know a little about me before I get too far into it. I grew up in Rochester, New York until the age of ten, then my family moved to Elmira, New York in 1972. The oldest of three, I eventually graduated from Notre Dame High School in 1980 and headed to St. John Fisher College in Rochester where I graduated with a BS in Economics in 1984. I am married to my wonderful wife Jackie and I have four children along with three grandkids.

I always loved to be of service to others. In 1980 I traveled to Kentucky in the dead of winter with a group called Glenmary to serve the most rural of people. I spent a summer while in college at the Office of Social Ministry in Elmira where I grew up, working in a soup kitchen, food cupboard and going from home to home to make sure those we served had enough clothing and food. After college I lived in Rochester and helped out at Blessed Sacrament Church's overnight shelter for a few years. Sometimes after working all day at my job, I would be asked to come sit at the shelter all night, then go back to work the following morning. It was exhausting, but gave 20 people a place to sleep. I was also a Big Brother to a kid (Jeff) from St. Joseph's Villa, an agency that serves troubled youths. I just loved being a friend to anyone in need.

Do you get the feeling I like to help others? I really do. I just love people. I loved the men at the overnight shelter, the mother desperate for food at the pantry, the guy in Kentucky so detached from current affairs that he had no idea who our president was, but could play a fiddle as well as anyone I know. These are the people I love in the world and strive to help. I am just drawn to people in these difficult situations. They need someone to just accept them for who they are or accept the situation they are in. I always loved how Jesus went to the lepers or ate with the sinners, those nobody else wanted to be with.

After the birth of Katy, my last child in 1998, I almost lost my wife. Her blood pressure spiked and she was admitted to the hospital. I remember the feeling of helplessness and praying to God for her to be okay. Eventually she recovered, but while sitting in the hospital, I felt my heart being tugged. Maybe it was being around all those doctors and nurses who were helping others, or all those I saw in need. I don't know which it was, but I began to think about wanting to do something more to help others, I missed that aspect of my life. I had become busy with my family, which was great, but I had a nagging feeling that I should be doing something else as well, so I began to pray about it.

It was while at Mass at St. Dominic Church in Shortsville New York when it hit me. We had a Deacon by the name of Ed Smith, and he used to give wonderful homilies that were very down to earth. I admired him and how he was able to share the Word of God in such basic terms. I talked to him and was told to talk to the head of Deacon Personnel, Deacon David Palma about exploring the possibility of becoming a Deacon.

I didn't know much about the Diaconate, so I made an appointment and we talked. I talked with my wife, and prayed about it. It felt right, yet

I wasn't completely comfortable with the idea. Still, I felt like I should apply. I filled out the paperwork, wrote a required autobiography, and after about five interviews and a psychological exam, I was accepted into the program. After all that, I felt like, okay, this MUST be what God wants, because it was a major hassle, and I went through it willingly. But questions still lingered.

I remember pulling out of my driveway for my first class, and my two little ones, Katy and Andy, were looking out the living room window at me waving goodbye. They were two and three years old at the time. I started to tear up thinking about how much of their growing up I would miss while going to school the next four years. I started to question myself more seriously from that moment on.

From my first class, I felt overwhelmed. This was a religion class and more with the history of the Catholic Church, encyclicals, canon law, learning the Bible. I felt like I knew nothing as I sat in the room with my six classmates and the highly educated teacher. This was going to be a challenge for me. I remember the very first paper I submitted about the mystics in the church; it was in a class with Sister Nancy Hawkins, who I really liked. I spent many hours on the paper trying to do a great job, only to have it returned to me and told it wasn't good enough and I needed to try again. My heart sank and the feeling that school was not for me only grew. I kept trying, looking at it as a challenge to be won. Eventually I did get through my first year. Great, now only three more to go. Sigh!

We did not get summers off from school, since we were required to do 80 hours of public service along with class. Each of us were assigned a place to serve, then write a couple papers of course and then share our experiences. I was assigned to Clifton Springs Hospital in the CPEP (Comprehensive Psychiatric Emergency Program) area. I knew I was in for a challenge when my first four hours were in a self-defense class. I was taught how to stand and prepare for the worst, flipping people over my shoulder or just tying to gain control over someone attacking me. Prior to this, running away always seemed to work since I was fast, but the instructor expected more apparently.

I had many experiences, to say the least, but there is one I will share here that was a exceptional learning moment for me. I was called down to the emergency room to interview a 14 year old boy who had just tried to commit suicide. Clifton Springs Hospital only admitted people age 18 and over, so I would have to find another hospital that would admit him after I was done with my initial interview.

As I read his chart before going into the room, I saw he was a pedophile. He was taken away from his parents and while in a foster home, he sodomized the foster family's young son. He later had a similar incident at another home. As I read on I could feel myself not liking this kid at all. It was right in the midst of news of priests being accused of this same behavior so it was an issue to which I was very sensitive. I walked into the room finding myself just wanting to do the job and get out.

As I entered the room I saw him lying on a stretcher, just looking up, emotionless. I'll call him Joe. He gave me a passing glance and just looked back to the ceiling. I introduced myself as I tried to hide the disdain for him I felt after having read his chart. I had a seven page report filled with questions to go through. As we started, he answered everything with no emotion.

When we moved to his family history, things began to get more emotional. He shared that he was taken away from his parents because his father sexually abused him and his mother did nothing about it for several years. Since then his parents had never tried to contact him. He had been placed with five different families but after sexually abusing others twice, he was placed in a home for juvenile delinquents. On this day, he tried to hang himself from a light fixture with his belt.

We continued to talk and eventually more of his story came out. He told me he had nobody, that he knew who he was and what he had done and that everyone hated him. "Nobody wants me, they all know my past and who I am. They all want to stay away from me, to not come near me, to avoid me". He looked me square in the eye and asked how I would feel to be hated, to not have anyone in this world love you. "I have no family, no friends, only people who work with me because it is their job. I don't know why I am like this. I hate myself. I want to die".

I had no answers, I had never met someone like Joe before. He shocked me like a slap in the face with his words. I had to admit I didn't like him because of what I had read and who he was. His assessment of how others saw him was totally right. But after hearing his story I started to feel compassion for him. I recall driving home that evening filled with anger at God. Why do You allow this stuff to happen God? Why do You allow so much hurt? Joe never had a chance, he was born into a bad situation and sexual abuse often leads to more sexual abuse. I couldn't hate Joe any longer, but I had so much emotion, I felt like I had to hate someone. Maybe Joe's dad? But what if Joe's father was also abused as a kid growing up? Who can I be mad at for this? I needed to focus my anger toward someone. God was the only one left for me.

I came back the next day and Joe was still there. Another staff member was trying to find a hospital elsewhere in the state that would accept him. She called hospitals from Buffalo to New York City with no success. "All the beds were full at this time," was the standard response, she was told to try back in six or twelve hours. So Joe remained there, on that stretcher waiting and waiting, thinking we would be moving him somewhere soon.

I decided to go say hello to Joe since he was still there and probably hadn't had any visitors. Sadly I was right, no one had come to visit him. The emergency room was packed and they had moved Joe from his room into the hallway that day. The nurse said the rooms were needed for privacy reasons. He was just lying there, not needing anything except a place to go.

I walked over to Joe and said "Hey Joe, how are you?" He just looked up with an expressionless look and said, "what do you think? They pushed me into the hallway and just left me here, tied to this stretcher. I thought I would have been gone by now." I explained to him that all the hospitals were full and we were still trying to find an open bed for him. He smirked and said, "Yeah right, c'mon, we both know nobody wants me." I thought he was probably right, but I made up the excuse that it was just busy and we had become overwhelmed last night with people and we'd soon get him squared away. He just looked up and didn't say anything. I squeezed his arm gently and walked away saying I would check on him later if he was still around. He had already been there for 14 hours so it couldn't be much longer, could it?

Well 14 hours ended up being 58 hours, lying on a stretcher in the ER. Over the next couple days, I visited him a number of times. The thought of him lying there all alone really bothered me. Nobody came to see or check on him the entire time. I really started to feel sorry for him and I could feel his hurt of having no one love him, so I made a special effort to go and just be with him. We talked about sports mostly, a little about school and people he hung around with at the center he was assigned but never about his family. Searching for things to say, I remember telling him about my first day at the hospital and how I was called out to visit a 68 year old lady who had stopped taking her medication. She was driving a riding lawnmower up and down the street, completely naked. It was the only time I saw him smile.

I was so angry with the system. He was right, no one wanted him. What a terrible thing to know at only 14 years old. I remember coming in the next day praying he was gone, yet kind of looking forward to seeing him. I had grown to like him. He was just a kid really except for his personal problems. I went directly to the ER to find he was gone, a place near Binghamton had finally accepted him. I was relieved, yet kind of sad as I had missed saying good bye to Joe. The nurse handed me a crumpled up piece of paper saying it was from that kid for me. I smirked and uncrumpled the sheet to find a short note. "Kevin, thank you for being my friend, Joe."

Those few words have been with me ever since. I always think about Joe when I start to get angry or upset with someone. Joe reminds me that I don't know the path another person has taken to get to this moment in life. Maybe if I walked in their shoes for a while, I would understand the why or how they are like they are. My life has been blessed, while others are born into situations they have no control over and suffer greatly. Joe taught me to think about the other person and try to realize they didn't come from where I did. They had a totally different path in life, one that may have brought great hurt and sadness along the way.

That little note also reminded me that I have much to offer, even if I don't see it in myself all the time. My experience with Joe convinced me to continue on with school. That just maybe God had plans for me I didn't know about yet. I sure never saw Joe coming! It is amazing how someone in our lives for such a short time can have such a big impact, if only we allow it and remain open to receiving it.

Beginning my second year of school, one of my classmates had been asked to leave the program bringing our class to six, including myself. It seemed that we were constantly asked to jump through hoops. Again I struggled, wanting so badly to do well, but never feeling like I was mastering the subjects. There was just too much to learn and understand. My classmates were all supportive as they shared their difficulties with me and the teachers were always supportive as well. The guys in my class were a perfect fit for me. They were easy going guys who also loved God and felt called to serve. They were a huge blessing to me throughout school and beyond, helping me in my times of struggle.

During the second semester, I took two classes that were real time burners; a counseling class and Hebrew Bible. I felt overwhelmed. As my spiritual director would tell me, I expected too much from myself. In the Bible class, I had to take a couple of verses from the Book of Samuel and write an exegesis on word origins, meanings, history, relevance to the New Testament, blah blah blah. I remember one person had a paper with 98 pages. Mine was "only" a 47 page paper that nearly broke me, and I only received a B on it. In the counseling class we paired up with a classmate and counseled each other on various problems we faced. I was teamed with my classmate and fellow deacon candidate Marty Hughes, a New York State trooper and just a great guy! Finding time to meet and then write was a real burden. We both had families, jobs, and just life to live, let alone all of this class work.

By Easter, I was on the verge of collapse again, I wanted out and I was going to leave after the semester was over. It was too much for me. I felt exhausted and defeated. I was in St. Dominic Church again where it all started for me, in front of the Blessed Sacrament on Holy Thursday night. I remember it like it was yesterday. Father Peter Clifford was to my left and my friend Lyn Butler in front to the left. I sat there praying to myself telling God I was sorry. Sorry I couldn't do it, sorry if I was letting Him down because I felt the calling to do it. I was full of self pity, feeling disappointed and overwhelmed. Then it happened. My spiritual director called it a moment of grace.

As I sat praying, I heard these words loud and clear, strong and loving "Kevin, do you love me?" My head popped up, my eyes wide open. Who said that? I looked around, but no one was looking at me or paying any attention to me. They were all in their own prayers. I was startled, God, is that you? I thought I was really losing it. That I'd gone crazy. I was hearing things. I had pushed myself too far. I am going to be a patient in the very hospital I worked at last summer. I went back to praying, feeling a bit unnerved as I listed my excuses for quitting the diaconate program. I was thinking that I was just not smart enough for the program. That there were so many people far smarter than me. Then it happened again. "Kevin, do you love me?" I looked around again but still nothing. It had to be God, what else could it be? I didn't think I was going nuts. I responded, "yes Lord, you know I do, but I continued with my excuses; I am scared to preach, any public speaking sends me into a panic, I can't do it." Then it happened a third time, "Kevin do you love me?"

I had to say yes, that I do love you God, very much. At that point I also understood in my heart that I had to continue with school. This isn't what I wanted to do. It was what God wanted me to do. I couldn't understand why God was calling me, with so many other people with so much more to offer. People who are great speakers and very intelligent people with great gifts to share. Why me? But I knew it was what God was asking of me and after all, I did love Him, so I decided I would continue, on the condition that it was up to God to get me through. I wasn't going to worry about it anymore. I just didn't have it in me. If He really wanted me to be a Deacon, He would get me through all of this. I waited for His affirmation with my conditions, but it never came. I still went forward, knowing I would just have to trust in God. He would have to take me by the hand and drag me kicking and screaming. I laughed to myself.

The next two years went much more smoothly. Thank you God! I spent that summer with Heritage Christian Services working with adults who had various disabilities. It was great and It was what I needed in my life. It was a summer of just loving and caring—and feeling loved back. I also learned a great deal about those who suffer from disabilities—mental, physical, emotional, or various combinations of them. I spent most of my time at one of the many group homes they operate, but also went to group activities like dances, amusement parks and ballgames. It was the first time I worked with people with developmental disabilities but it was an invaluable experience.

During my third year of school things were much easier, I learned to not worry so much about grades and focused on learning all I could. If I was meant to get through this and be accepted as a Deacon, it would happen. I didn't want to do it anymore, but I knew God was calling me to it. If He wanted me to be a Deacon, He would lead me through it. I just kept wondering, why me? My biggest disappointment during the year was my friend, Marty, decided to leave the program. He discerned that he was not being called to be a Deacon. I understood, of course, but still I missed him very much. I felt close to Marty having gone through that counseling class together and sharing our various struggles. One of the other guys in the program suffered a heart attack during class and decided to drop out of the program. We were now down to four.

The last year of classes went fairly well. We visited churches to learn how to perform baptisms, weddings, and adorations. The Pastor at St. Dominic's Church was Fr. John Gagnier and he allowed me to start giving reflections from the pulpit during Mass. I was facing one of my biggest fears, preaching, but I knew I had to do it. I was terrible and I knew it. I was petrified with fear, but for the most part the community was very supportive of me. I had a few people complain to the Bishop about my preaching and not being ordained yet, but Father Gagnier always stuck by and supported me. I even had one woman pull me out of line as I professed out after Mass one day. She yelled at me about how bad I was and how she disapproved of my sermon. She totally missed my message and misunderstood my point, so it was a nice reminder that sometimes people hear things differently then I intended. I needed to be more careful.

I still remain very thankful to the parish community of St. Dominic's. They have always been there for me. They put up with a guy full of doubt and questions all along the way, trying to overcome his fears. They were wonderful about it. I never really called a parish my home, but St. Dominic's in Shortsville will always be a most special parish in my heart. It was there where I first felt called.

My last summer course was spent in downtown Rochester at Saints Peter and Paul Church on Main Street. It was an old, large church with amazing artwork all around. The first time I entered it I was surprised to see half of the pews ripped out from the back of it. It was just a big space. I loved the magnifiance and beauty of the church; the paintings, statues, stained glass windows. But the real beauty of this church was it's people.

It was a different church to which I was accustomed. It was a smaller, shrinking parish community as many former member families had moved away from the inner city. During the Sign of Peace, everyone left their seat and walked around to shake hands and hug each other. I loved that aspect and how it allowed me meet everyone. It took 5 or 10 minutes sometimes for the sign of peace, but it was community, like a true family coming together. I also loved at the end of Mass, people from the street would come in and we would form a large prayer circle in the space where the pews were removed. After we prayed together, tables full of bread and food were brought out and passed to those in need.

I also became quite involved with St. Peter's Kitchen, a food cupboard offering lunches to the community during the week. We served about 170 meals each day and it was a great way for me to learn about the people in the inner city of Rochester. I actually had the opportunity to serve on the Board of Directors for a couple years, from 2010-2012.

While school was a bumpy ride at times, it was a great learning experience, a real journey. I am NO scholar, that's for sure. I am not a great speaker and I really had nothing special to offer. I was just an average guy who felt called by God to serve in the role of a Deacon. My classmates were great and I give them credit for helping me get through this program. It continues to amaze me how God took care of me the whole way. If I look at the class of candidates ahead of me or behind me, I don't think I would have completed the schooling necessary to get my masters degree and eventually become ordained. Dave LaFortune, Joe Placious and Wil Johnson were all like me in many ways, true brothers. We used to joke about how could the Diocese could let the four of us into this program. We felt like a misfit class in the midst of it all. I think the gifts we shared was not being overly serious and having the ability to laugh at ourselves as a group. Together we continued on, eventually all being ordained on May 21, 2005.

It was a beautiful ceremony. I was overcome with joy and humbled. However the question still hung over me. "What does God have in store for me?" I had no objective other than to serve and do God's will, but what was that?

For my first Mass I was allowed to serve as a Deacon at my home parish of St. Dominic's. I was especially blessed as my two youngest children, Andy and Katy, celebrated their First Communion. After that Mass, I waited to be assigned by the diocese.

A couple weeks later, I was asked to go talk to Fr. Robert Bourcy at St. Patrick's in Macedon New York. What a great guy; we hit it off immediately. It turned out that when he was ordained a priest, his first assignment was in Ithaca, New York serving with my Uncle Fr. Bernie Carges who was pastor of Immaculate Conception Church at the time. Fr. Rob and I found it very ironic at the time and both felt that maybe my Uncle Bernie was bringing us together. It was also interesting that the day we met was my Uncle's birthday, June 3rd. While I had always looked forward to serving with my uncle, unfortunately I never had the chance as my Uncle Bernie passed away while I was studying to become a deacon.

Fr. Rob was very welcoming and great to work with, a real friend to me. The community of Macedon was also very supportive, friendly, and I loved being a part of it. I think what I loved most was they were not overly serious when I messed up and were very understanding while I "learned the ropes" of being a Deacon. They were patient and I very quickly fell in love with the community.

Immediately I began serving as Deacon at St. Patrick's Church. I loved presiding at baptisms, funerals, weddings, and even preaching became more comfortable. I also found out that I wouldn't enjoy all aspects of this new ministry of mine. In fact there was something I grew quickly to dislike, and that was meetings. Meetings about liturgy, finance council, parish council, staff meetings, and worst of all, the meetings about clustering with two other churches, St. Anne's in Palmyra and St. Gregory's in Marion.

While certain parts of being a Deacon were very fulfilling, I certainly did not like other aspects. I was starting to think and began praying, asking God, is this it? You called me to this ministry, is this what you want of me? Then about a year into my ministry I was contacted by Deacon Bill Coffey and asked if I wanted to go to Jamaica to serve the poor for a week. I thought it would be a great opportunity and it played into what I loved doing most, serving those in need.

I had never been to Jamaica, or any developing country for that matter, but I had seen pictures and read stories. I had been in the heart of

Rochester in soup kitchens and overnight shelters for years. I honestly thought this would be an interesting experience more than anything else. Little did I know my life was about to change and God was about to reveal His plan for me after all those years.

THIS IS JAMAICA?

It was cold, snowy and grey when I left Rochester for Jamaica in 2006. Flying into Kingston Jamaica for my week of missionary work was exciting. Looking out the window of the plane as we descended, the waters were so clear and inviting, the hills and mountains full of greenery. I understood why Jamaica was such a tourist attraction, with it's amazing beauty.

We landed, got off the plane, and were welcomed by sun and heat. Ahh, I felt like I was going to really love it there just for the weather alone. We went through customs, gathered our luggage and headed off on a bus to our hotel. There were about twelve or thirteen of us, three other Deacons from the Diocese of Rochester and then people from around the country. I was traveling with Food for the Poor, a group that served those in need in the Caribbean and Latin America.

Fr. Paul our guide immediately started to teach us about the island. My biggest surprise was that I thought tourism was the largest income generator for the island of 2.7 million people, I soon learned it is third. Remuneration, or people who leave the country and send money back to family members, is the largest source of funds for Jamaica. Second, and very critical to my later thinking, is the mining of bauxite (aluminum ore). The mining industry is the largest source of employment for the residents of Jamaica.

So there I was, riding along on the bus, learning about the country. When my real learning began started in Riverton, a landfill in Kingston, Jamaica, the largest on the island. We have landfills in America so I wasn't sure why this particular landfill was worthy of talking about. As I soon found out, Riverton would be something that haunts my thoughts and probably will forever.

Imagine if you can—A large pit, a couple square miles I would guess, filled with garbage. There's more. It's full of people, thousands of people. Fr. Paul began to tell us the story as I began to lose the joy that filled me just moments earlier.

People of all ages were picking through garbage, looking for food, things to sell or use, perhaps something that could fill a hole in the place they called home. People were living in makeshift pieces of wood, metal, or whatever worked, homes that are right there in the landfill because they have nowhere else to go. I am sick to my stomach from the stench of garbage in the heat. I can taste the sweat rolling down my face, and the dirt and smoke in the air. Bugs are flying all about. Rats, lizards, snakes and birds are mixed in the very filth where moms, dads and children are digging in hopes of finding something. Two young boys find part of something that they break in two and eat. A garbage truck pulls in and dozens of people run to it. Father. Paul tells us maybe it is from a resort and there will be leftover food in it, which is the best garbage.

It was so beautiful looking down as we flew in to Jamaica. Soon after the sun and warmth embraced me. Only an hour later, I feel like I am in hell. I am literally standing at the gates of hell as I learn how my brothers and sisters must pick through garbage to survive.

I quickly learn that the people of Jamaica have no government services like we do; they are left to fend for themselves. Sometimes the only place left for the poorest and most vulnerable is the landfill. I am thankful we are not staying here but simply driving by to witness.

THE MUSTARD SEED

Upon arriving at the Mustard Seed, I was immediately shocked upon walking into the all cement room. The cinder block walls, concrete floors, and dark blue and pink paint chipped colors. The smell was a combination of urine and bleach, and seemed so dark to me. It was dark yet simultaneously full of life. Children from as young as five up to

fifteen years of age, all lying in beds or sitting in wheel chairs numbering close to forty or fifty. Some were silent, while some did all they could to get my attention. They were moaning, crying, screaming, arm waving, calling out to me, and some laughing and smiling as I glanced in their direction. There were so many in a small, cramped space, all with some sort of physical challenge or disability. Rows and rows of children, to my left and to my right. I was filled with self doubt, why was I here? What should I do? Where do I start? What have I gotten myself into? This was so different than any other room of children I had ever walked into. They were packed in like sardines. The group of twelve people I was with began to move about with trepidation as we took in what was before

us. I moved to my left, towards a row of wheelchairs. The first few children did not respond to my greeting. Blank stares returned my hello. Then I met David. His strained smile greeted me as I moved closer to say hello. As I knelt down I was then touched on the arm by Steven who was in the next chair. Steven was trying to grab my hand but couldn't quite master the action. I put my hand in his and you could see the joy on his face. It was like God welcoming me to Jamaica. Neither David or Steven could speak, but as I spoke to them, we held hands the whole time. I could tell by the look in their eyes and their managed grins, that we were communicating on a much deeper level.

One of the three staff members told me some of the children's stories, how they ended up here. Most, if not all, were abandoned by their families. Some were found in the street, others brought here directly. I questioned what she meant by this and she explained they were abandoned because their families could not afford to care for all their children, especially a child with physical and mental challenges. You see, in Jamaica children are expected to contribute to the family to survive, and these children cannot. If you are poor here in Jamaica, in order for these children to survive, parents sometimes have to choose which children they will keep and which ones they must give up. There is not always enough food or medicine for everyone, and having no support from the government, it is in some ways survival of the fittest. Sometimes parents can't bear the choice of who to feed and who not to, or worse

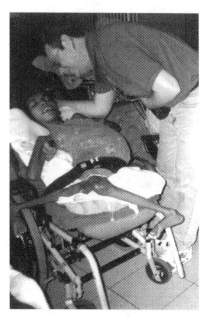

yet, let die. As a result they take their child and leave them somewhere in hopes someone will find them and care for them. They feel it is the only hope. I couldn't believe what I was hearing as I listened, unable to comprehend what I had just heard in my own mind. Those sentences jolted me hard, I was numbed and in shock, thinking of my own children. What if I had to choose? I immediately thanked God for never putting me in such a situation. I looked back at the boys as they showed their excitement at my being there as they continued to hold my hand best they could. They seemed so happy, so happy to have someone to hold and give them

attention. The staffer went on to say that "this visit would be the highlight of their month." She explained how they try to give all the children enough love and attention, but it isn't an easy task. Between bathing, changing and feeding the children, there is so much need. "We are giving care, safety and love to children but they know we work here. Visitors like you come to be with them, and the kids know it." The love

we were giving that day was so desperately needed and desired. The children knew we came to see them and they loved our presence. I looked back to David and Steven, and hugged them tightly. After taking a picture together, I said goodbye, and I walked over to the bed areas.

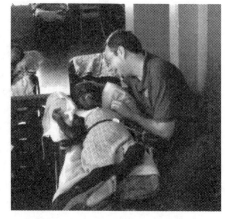

I stopped to wipe some tears from my eyes. I was feeling devastated, like I was kicked in the stomach or knocked in the head. All the while thinking and wondering, how could this be? I began to ask God over and over, why? I turned to a row of beds and put on a happy face. I had no time to think and reflect, I was just enjoying some time with these precious angels for now. A row of six or seven beds, all with little girls in them, with limbs that were thin and contorted awaited me. Most could not move or speak, communicating by grunts, groans and sometimes a smile. I greeted them by looking directly at them, smiling or brushing the hair out of their eyes and telling them all how beautiful they are. The second to last little girl whose name was Melinda in the row smiled broadly at me, so I sat on the bed next to her. Her body was badly contorted and there seemed to be no muscles in her limbs, only skin and bones. The girl to the right of her had a broad smile also, she had an enlarged head, too big for her body. She could not talk, but her tiny giggles were contagious. A staff member explained to me that she suffered from hydrocephalus, or "water on the brain", a condition which is treatable in developed countries. She never had a chance for treatment, based solely on where she was born. Her caretaker explained to me that comfort is a major goal in caring for these children, but not all of these

children can be saved, due to the cost of medical treatment. I looked back at this little girl, and there she was still smiling at me, with no idea what I had just been told. She was just so happy for me to be there. I told her she was beautiful, and stroked her hair as I took in her loving smile. After a few minutes I glanced to my right and saw another wheelchair, off to the side, separated from 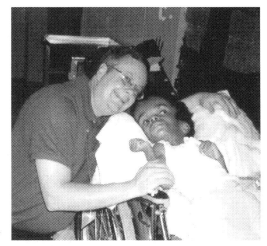 the others. I felt like I needed to go over there for some reason so I gave Melinda and her friend a kiss on the forehead, said good bye, and walked towards the chair.

This little girl also had hydrocephalus. I was told this develops because their mothers are malnourished during the first trimester of their pregnancy. I thought to myself how this could so easily be prevented, by just providing a healthy diet to moms during their pregnancy. I was angered by this as well, how some of these children suffer only because of lack of food. I began to question God again in my mind about why this has to happen. I could feel my anger at God rising as I looked at this little girl who I called Angel. I asked one of the staff women why she was isolated from the others? Sadly I was informed partly because of lack of space, but mostly because she was close to death. I was taken aback by her words and beside myself already filled with emotion!! With tears filling my eyes as I listened, I turned away so no one could see them. The woman put her hand on my shoulder to comfort me and reassure me that this little one would not suffer much more. Soon she would be free, and back in heaven with God. I looked back at Angel and she was expressionless. She was unable to frown or smile anymore, she could only moves her eyes back and forth. She looked at me and then, I broke down again as much as I tried not to and remain strong. Here I was, trying to offer comfort, friendship, love or anything positive yet I was consumed with a feeling of emptiness and desperation of what I was feeling inside. I knelt down next to her and lightly sobbed as my tears fell upon her, as it was too much for me. This innocent child who had suffered her whole life was abandoned by her family, and was now on the verge of dying, all because her mother possibly didn't have enough to eat. Emotions ripped through me: sadness, anger, a constant questioning of why. I needed to know why God. Why did she have to suffer like this? I spent the rest of my time there, holding her hand and stroking her head, trying to smile and talk to her, while holding back my tears. All I could do was look into her deep brown eyes and love her.

Deacon Leo Aman came over to me as I knelt next to her bed, probably seeing me struggling, unable to hide my emotions. I told him her story, and asked him too, why was life so unfair to these children? I was desperate for answers, I was hurting so bad. He explained that "only God knows, but it is clear by your emotions and how she has gotten to you, that you were meant to be here, to meet her, be with her and know her story. Maybe God created her in part—to reach you and touch your heart. Every person has a purpose and serves God in their own way and with the gifts they are given. Perhaps you aren't here for her, but rather, she is here for you? I looked back down at her as Leo placed his hand on my shoulder. What are you telling me Angel?

I heard Angel died about two weeks after my visit. It broke my heart but I was happy for her to be back in heaven with God. As I looked back on it months later I think Deacon Leo was exactly right. I think God was talking to me through Angel. Funny how this little girl who couldn't talk, smile, move or communicate in any way, except to look into my eyes, began to set the path for the rest of my life as a Deacon. I feel as though her eyes were God's eyes looking back into mine and telling me why He called me to the diaconate and that I was needed here in some fashion.

It's funny how I never wanted to be a Deacon, never knew why I had such a strong calling for it. But after I came back from Jamaica in 2006, it was the gift of the people and their stories, these little children and especially Angel that showed me where God needed me to somehow serve. By the passion in my heart for the people I had met in Jamaica, I began to figure out why I was called to be a Deacon perhaps, where God wanted me all along. One of my many "Why God?" questions was beginning to be answered, but I still wasn't sure how He wanted me to go about it yet. "Great", I thought, now God gave me a "How?" question.

THE VILLAGE

We pulled into a small group of homes in what seemed like the middle of nowhere. How did we ever find this place, I thought. We had been off the main road for about five miles and seen nothing but dirt since. Big rutted holes had tossed us around for 30 minutes, and I was anxious to get off the small bus we rode. As we exited, a group of children ran to the door to greet us. They were all smiles and filled with excitement. A few older people slowly strode over as I smiled at the kids and began saying hello.

They were so happy, just like Christmas I thought, as they were jumping, yelling, and running around. I later learned a few groups had come by before and shared candy with them, and they assumed we had some to pass out also and of course I did! It is one of my favorite things to do when in a developing country with the kids.

I started to walk toward one of the homes and a girl of about 12 ran out of nowhere with a big bucket of water. Her name was Claire. She put the five-gallon bucket down quickly and ran over to me. She wanted me to take her picture, which I did. Then she ran to me and asked to see it on the digital camera. I learned later they had no mirrors so this was a rare chance for her to see herself. I immediately thought about my daughters—how would they ever survive without looking at themselves for a day, let alone months!

I asked her about the water and what it was for. It turns out it was for everything: to drink, wash themselves, their few clothes, and a few plants they were growing for food. She explained it was her duty to get the water each day, maybe three times a day when it was really dry due to lack of rain. She was lucky today because it had rained pretty hard last night, so she hoped to make only one trip today. She went on to explain that it took about an hour and 20 minutes to fill it each time by walking to a river on the other side of the hill. Getting there is much faster when the bucket is empty, she was happy to tell me. All I could think about was this little 12-year-old carrying five gallons of water for over a mile back home.

She took me to her home, a big house with four doors on each side. The first door was where her family lived. It was a room about 10 x12 feet, at most. It had a queen-size bed and a chest of drawers. All together, five people lived here. Usually her mother and two younger sisters got to sleep in the bed, while she and her dad got the floor most nights, what little floor there was. I was embarrassed when I turned around and noticed three pairs of shoes on the step just outside the door, and those inside had taken off their shoes, except for me. I apologized, stepped back outside the door as Claire and her mom laughed. "You are our guest," the mom said and she invited me back in.

We chatted for about five minutes about life in Jamaica and all she wanted to talk about was how blessed she and her family were, and how I was part of their blessing. I found that hard to believe because I was just a guest visiting and they were so kind to invite me into their home. She continued to talk and went on to say "God has brought you here to hear our stories, to see our need, to know we are here, to answer our prayers. Our government doesn't come, nobody from the big city come, nobody listen or care about us except God—and now you and your group. You come from United States to my home—and you listen. God brought you here. Thank you."

I never thought of it like that before. True, I wanted to see, learn and understand—but that was me and what I wanted. I guess it turned the tables around a little on me and I was there for more than just my wants or desires. I was there to listen, see, touch, smell, and take in as much as I could—but then what? Just know about it? Just be aware of what is here and know that Jamaica isn't just a paradise like I've seen in TV commercials? I was still trying to figure out what Angel was telling me from the Mustard Seed the other day. All I could do was go with the flow for now, no time to think and reflect, just take things in.

Claire wanted to show me around so she took me to where she washed her clothes. I took a few more pictures and met a few other people. I was having so much fun interacting with everyone. They enjoyed the company of our group as much as we enjoyed being there. Then around a group of trees, there it was. There stood a house that looked as though it could

collapse any second. I saw a young boy chasing a chicken and a little girl of about four or five standing totally naked. I walked over and a young woman waved hello and smiled. I waved back and introduced myself.

She was getting ready to give her children baths in this little yellow tub. I asked if I could take some pictures and look around. She called into the house and her mother, Monica, came out. After explaining who I was, they began to share their stories with me. This was a far more difficult story to listen to.

Apparently, the kid's dad had been arrested for stealing fruit from some private land. He had been put in jail for 30 days or so. She explained their children were starving and needed to eat something. "My daughter is sick and we have no medicine. But we must buy food first and hope she gets better. It is all we have—our faith in God to deliver us from these problems." I looked at the little girl and saw her runny nose and she also seemed to have a bad eye. All the kids were so skinny, except for their bellies, which is a sign of malnourishment, parasites, or infections in their liver.

The grandmother invited me into their home as the mom finished washing the youngest son. I was sick and heartbroken all at the same time. This was a home, I thought? People live here? This wasn't safe for a dog to be in let alone three little children and some adults. Honestly I was scared to step inside for fear of getting hurt, but the kids ran ahead and the grandmother didn't hesitate, so I figured it must be okay.

Inside was a mattress on the floor and some drawers where they kept things. It was still dark in spite of the holes in the roof and walls. It smelled damp and dirty from the rain the night before, almost moldy. I didn't know how this place stayed together, and I was a little worried to be inside. Nails jutted out everywhere as well as pieces of wood or sheet metal. It seemed like mosquitoes followed me and there were bugs crawling in and out of some of the holes. The holes were so big I thought—what else comes in here at night?

Monica told me it was a good day to wash the clothes and the kids because everything was already wet from last night's rain. "We all gather in the driest corner of the house when it rains, but we still get wet," she said. "But we are blessed because our home keeps the wind off us and much of the rain. God is great."

As I turned around in the midst of my disbelief from what I was seeing to agree with her, she dropped to her knees and started crying. She looked at me and started to thank God for me and my coming to her. "We pray to God always for help, and He has sent you here to us. Please help us," she cried. I was speechless! I didn't know what to say. I stood there for what seemed like minutes searching for words, and then I did

the only thing I could think of. I walked over and hugged her, and said,
"I will try. I will pray to God for you and your family." She wept on my shoulder a little and said thank you over and over. She got back on her knees and thanked God again for sending me, for hearing their prayers. She said I was proof God was hearing their prayers and that I had renewed their faith and given them hope!

I walked out of the home not knowing what to think. Maybe she was just crazy? Had I strayed too far from the group? I was scared and I wanted to get away. It was overwhelming, to say the least. I took a few more pictures and walked back over to the group. The need was so great and I had nothing to offer I thought. I felt scared and helpless, not knowing what to do or say.

That chance meeting had given me a feeling of uneasiness. Maybe it was the grandmother dropping to her knees like that and crying and thanking God for my presence. Or maybe it was because the house was so bad, far worse than I could have imagined on my own. Perhaps it was those three kids who were so hungry and sick. Maybe it was because Monica forced me to think—was I actually here for a reason other than to experience a developing country for myself and to be aware? Is there more to all this? Why are these people touching my hearts so much God? Why more than all the others I have served in soup kitchens and shelters at home in America?

There were too many questions . . . I was felt exhausted with all the questions in my head. I was numb by just how bad it actually was here for some people in this island paradise. I was scared by that Grandmother saying that I was answering her prayers by my being there, I gave her hope. I had never felt like I was the answer to anyone's prayer before. Was God trying to tell me something? Okay, I was here answering her prayer, but I don't have any answers God, now what? This is where you take over God, it is too much for me to handle.

I remember coming home and pulling into my driveway after the trip. I sat in the car for a minute just looking at my modest home. It wasn't perfect; it needs some work here and there, but wow, how different than the home I was in just days earlier. The roof was solid, it didn't leak, and there were no holes in the walls. I could walk in, flick a switch and lights would come on. If I took a few steps to the left I could go into the kitchen with cupboards full of food, and a few steps more, running water! I didn't have to hike three miles today with a five gallon bucket to brush my teeth or get a drink and the water was clean to boot! I would see my family and thank God that I am blessed to be able to feed them, give them an education, take them to a doctor if they get sick. I also thought about how blessed I was to be born to such wonderful parents who loved me so much and could provide for me growing up. How blessed I was to have an education, a job and the opportunity to live in America.

Yes, I sat there and just couldn't stop thinking about how blessed I was. Maybe that was what God was trying to show me, how many gifts he has shared with me. At that moment I couldn't stop saying thank you to God for all I had, for all I had been given. I couldn't say thank you enough. I had never realized how blessed I was until I pulled into that driveway and saw my house, my family, all healthy, warm, and fed. God is great, like Monica had told me! But what about Monica? And those three little kids and their parents? What were they doing tonight? I imagine they were thanking God for their blessings also, perhaps that they had food today, or their dad came home, or maybe something as simple as, they were alive for another day.

BACK HOME

As I settled back into my normal life, I would look at my pictures of the trip, so disappointing to me. They were missing something, not telling the whole story. And even when I told the stories, I was never satisfied with how I delivered them. I just could not convey how bad things were, I just don't think people grasped how bad it was. It was difficult to live with what I knew and not know how to express it fully so others could understand.

About 6 months later, I was in Ithaca, NY and stopped by the cemetery to visit my Uncle Bernie's grave. He was a priest in the Diocese of Rochester and had passed away a couple years earlier. I really missed him as we used to talk a lot about God and the priesthood. The trip to Jamaica was still heavy on my mind. I had seen so many things and I was devastated by what I took in still . . . the gravity of the need. It was far worse than I could have imagined, just so foreign to my senses that people hurt and suffered so much. I had no idea. This was a trip that not only touched my heart, but changed it forever.

I wished he was here to talk to but I felt better having a good cry with him thinking about all I had witnessed. It had taken months for it all to sink in and for my disbelief to disappear and accept the reality of what was! I thought to myself, okay, now I need to tell people these stories. I need to start sharing what I saw. I just didn't know how, how could I make people understand just how bad some people are forced to live.

I began to realize that maybe God didn't just send me to realize how blessed I was—but maybe to start actually sharing my blessings. Maybe to tell the stories of people I met and to share the situations people must endure in foreign lands sometimes. How we take for granted so much here because we just don't know any better. Even when I have helped people down on their luck, there was always a government to turn to offering food assistance, unemployment, Medicaid, etc. These people in

Jamaica had nowhere to turn but to their actual neighbor who may or may not be able to help. Right now more than 2.5 billion people live on less than $2 a day in this world and nearly 11 million children under five die in developing countries. Sixty percent of them die from malnutrition and hunger related diseases.

Yes, I knew the statistics but now . . . I knew some of the people. I had seen it firsthand and it changed my life forever. I had to do something to try and help Monica and her family. I had to at least try. After all, she told me I was her hope. I now understood what they were telling me in that little community of homes in Jamaica. Maybe God had sent me to meet them and hear their stories, but now I began to understand that God was sending me to serve them. God was listening to their prayers, and I was sent to hear them also, like he sends all of us somewhere to help and serve.

We all have a calling in life and I was finally beginning to realize mine while sitting in a cemetery with my Uncle Bernie. I realized I had to do something, knowing what I now knew and saw, the reality of life some people must live. How many other people are there that don't realize or understand like I failed to before I went to see for myself. I had to stop being frustrated and start acting, start doing something, but what?

It had been about a year since my trip and I was still wrestling with the "how" question. I decided that maybe I should share my stories and ask for money to help the people I had met. It was the thing I hated most, asking for money, but my heart ached so bad for those people I met and I had to do something. I decided I needed help, a professional money raiser, so I called my friend Rod Christian.

Rod was a college buddy and worked in donor relations at some large non-profits in the Rochester area. We met for lunch and I told him my goal and how I needed help. Through this came Deacon Kevin's Circle of Friends. I created a website www.deaconkevin.org where I put up pictures of my trip. The website is still up with some pictures if you want to see a few more.

Anyhow I began to raise money through my site to build a tilapia fish farm. We could grow fish which could be used as food and the excess sold for money to buy other necessities. I needed $25,000 so I began, calling newspapers, churches, civic groups, anyone who might listen in the hopes they would donate to my fund.

It was slow, too slow for my liking. I would get $300 here or $25 there, never really making the progress I hoped. But I kept at it and accepted it that this was what God wanted of me for now.

But God wasn't done with me yet, I was asked to go visit the country of Haiti which I had heard was even worse off than Jamaica. I accepted the opportunity and off I went with eyes and heart wide open.

WELCOME TO HAITI

I had heard that Haiti was the poorest country in the Western Hemisphere and after what I witnessed in Jamaica, I couldn't imagine things being much worse . . . but they were. As soon as you fly into the country you realize this isn't a very nice place. A former French colony, Haiti was the first country to gain emancipation in the world, but there was a cost. France wanted all the country's lumber, so most of the trees were cut down leaving mountains and hills with no trees at all. Along with the price of freedom came the price of being excluded by the rest of the world as other countries were fearful their slaves would get the idea of wanting freedom as well. So Haiti was avoided by most other countries wanting to trade. It was the beginning of what would cause Haiti to become the poorest country on this side of the planet.

It doesn't take you long to see what they mean as one of the first things you notice is garbage seemingly everywhere. Piles of it everywhere, in the streets, in the canals, in every direction you turn. The only beautiful spot was by the capital where everything for five blocks was fairly clean. After that however, it is a mess, and that was before the earthquake in 2010.

Wherever I went, my heart ached for the people I met. They were happy with life and thankful to God for what they had, but they were also aware of how badly they were hurting. In 2012, the unemployment rate was over 40% and literacy stood at 52.9%. I have read under employment numbers as high as 86% in this country of 9.8 million people who are in desperate need.

I traveled there six months before the earthquake, in fact the hotel I stayed at was totally destroyed and 56 people lost their lives in it. Things are worse now, but even before that, it was beyond belief.

The difficult part of traveling to Haiti for me is they speak a form of French called Creole, which I don't know so I am always at the mercy of a translator. Our first day there we went to a health clinic run by nuns from Montreal Canada in the heart of Port Au Prince. The waiting line starts in the middle of the night to see the two doctors who come to see patients and when we arrived around 11am there must have been at least 150 people waiting. I later went to a hospital where I was able to lay my hands on and pray for three lepers, just like Jesus did some 2000 years ago.

We spent one afternoon at a soup kitchen scooping three ladles of rice and one ladle of broth into the buckets the people would bring. The soup kitchen back home in Rochester I helped at once in a while fed about 170 a day. Today the lines for this place stretched for several blocks and it was estimated by the staff they would feed close to 10,000 people in conjunction with a few other kitchens nearby. Sadly this is the only meal most of them will have all day. The kitchen starts serving food at 10am and goes for several hours each day. Everyone knows the routine and there were no issues today, but the kitchen employs armed guards to keep the peace. This number has climbed to over 20,000 since the earthquake in 2010.

I would have to say the most difficult thing about this trip for me was my visit to the Citi Soliel—or in English, Sun City. It is one of the most impoverished and densely populated areas in the world. We first stopped into a school where the children sang us a couple songs and then we took some pictures and just had fun. One boy asked to feel my hair so I took off my hat and next thing I knew there were 20 kids rubbing their hands in my hair wanting to feel it. Lucky for me I still had some. They were also rubbing my arms wondering if I was covered in powder or something to make me so white.

The school is simply a big building with sections on either side which are used as classrooms. When the school was built there was a large chain link fence all around it. For those children not fortunate enough to go to school, they would stand outside the fence looking in all day. A large cement wall had to be built around it to stop the other kids from staring in and causing a distraction to the children lucky enough to attend.

After the school day started, we went outside the gates to meet some of the people who live in the city and get a first hand view of life here. From the pictures you can see it is terrible, scraps of zinc, stones, wood thrown together as best as possible to create a home. Gangs are a big problem here and people are beaten, robbed of what little they have, and the women are often raped. The desperation of the situation has everyone in survival mode, living one day to the next.

Rape was so prevalent, it was not against the law until 2005. As a result of rape, many young girls have babies and as of today, 1 out of 15 children will not live to age five due to lack of food, water and medicine. This sounds bad, and it is, but just ten years ago is was 1 in 9, so progress is being made. It was tough to have my picture taken with so many kids and think about which ones wouldn't survive another year here. It was the closest thing to hell on this planet that I have ever witnessed.

We were invited into peoples "homes" and the translator did his best to accurately translate, but it was a bit chaotic as we were creating a real scene as "rich Americans" were here. As word spread, our guide became increasingly worried and wanted us to leave before anyone of the gangs arrived and threatened us for money or tried to kidnap us. Apparently we would bring a good ransom. I was able to get some pictures with the kids. It was such a treat for them that they knocked me to the ground trying to catch a glimpse of themselves on my camera. I loved their enthusiasm, and we laughed as I tried to get up with nine or ten children helping me.

One girl of about thirteen or fourteen I would guess was trying to get me to come with her, but I kept refusing because of the situation. She kept talking to me but I didn't understand. When the translator finally got a chance to talk to me I asked him to ask the girl what she wanted? I assumed she wanted me to go to her place to see her home and show me something about her community. What I found out was she was trying to prostitute herself in exchange for $2. I thought the translator was joking but I could see he was serious as the girl continued to tug on my arm. She was so young, my heart sank as low as it ever has at that very moment. I asked the translator to question her if she was worried about contracting HIV. She responded while shaking her head no as she explained she could live for years if she got that, but her family needed food now to live

this week. My heart sank even lower. I looked at her and her face was all business, so serious. I tried to hug her, but she backed away thinking I was trying to take advantage of her. The guide wondered if she had previously been a victim of rape. At thirteen I was in junior high school, riding my bike, going to baseball games. this girl was trying to survive another week. Life was so unfair to so many, especially here in this slum.

I was at the point I get to sometimes where I just couldn't see anymore. Again the hurt and suffering was more than my mind could accept, but it wasn't over. I had two more things God wanted me to see and know about as I started to lose control of my emotions again just wanting to sit down and cry at all I had seen. We had done a circle of some homes and we passed an area that had no homes but had puddles of water and smelled incredibly bad, not that any of this area smelled nice, but this spot was particularly bad. I don't know why but I, until now, had not noticed there were no sewers here. Maybe I just assumed there would be being a city, but no, there was nothing. These homes only had pots to use when relieving themselves, which were brought to this spot and dumped out. The poorest of the poor lived closest to these various dumping spots all over the city. I felt nauseous and wanted to throw up while the kids laughed and played around me. Their happiness kept me going.

Before getting on the bus, I needed to horse around with these children for a few minutes to forget about what I had just seen, if even for one minute. I needed them and their smiles. They were showing me some of their toys. An empty pop bottle half filled with dirt to create a rattle. A plastic grocery bag with a piece of string tied to it to make a kite. A milk carton pushed in the dirt, pretending it was a truck. Then I saw what I thought were mud pies on a table. I told the translator we all make mud pies all over the world when we are kids. But they weren't mud pies at all, he called them mud cookies. It was explained to me that sometimes when there is no food for days, the mothers will take mud and try to mix it with something like butter, a bouillon cube or salt for flavor, dry them in the sun and then feed them to the children to ease the hunger pains. The mothers weep knowing their children are starving and cannot bear the crying so they feed the children these to fill their stomachs.

All I could think was, how is this allowed to happen in our world? We can do so many amazing things. Technology has brought us so far, but the children I am hugging today will have only dirt to eat tonight. How could this be? And again the questions raced through my heart and mind, how God can this be permitted to happen in our world? Do something!

LITTLE CHILDREN OF JESUS

Did you ever go someplace and just feel life was perfect? Like you could stay forever and be happy? I think about the ballplayer in the movie Field of Dreams, Shoeless Joe Jackson asking—"is this heaven"? Well of course nothing is perfect here in this world, but sometimes we get that feeling or a taste of something so special we might just have a quick thought that wow, maybe this is what heaven might be like.

I know we all have our own ideas, but if you believe in God, then you know that God is love in simplest terms. "That God so loved the world, He gave his only son." (John 3:16)

Being in Haiti was anything but heaven and I was hurting badly in my heart, knowing firsthand the suffering of the people here. I was sick to my stomach, my mind still trying to accept the reality of what my senses had taken in the past few days. I always tell people to see pictures and read stories is one thing, but when all your senses are under attack from something so bad, it changes you, sometimes forever.

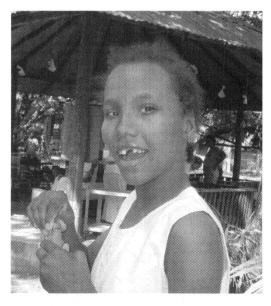

It was here where I met Gladys. In the midst of this country, which is in the worst condition in the entire Western Hemisphere I found a piece of heaven, an orphanage called the Little Children of Jesus Home.

I remember pulling up to the walled-in facility. The

poverty was incredible in Haiti, far worse than anything I had ever seen before, but as the gates opened and we pulled into the orphanage, it was beautiful. A nice, big house with plants and flowers, with three or four children who came out to greet us. I was the first one off the bus and I was immediately hugged tightly by this girl of about 12 years old. She had a great smile and held me tight and wouldn't let go. As we walked around to the back, I was shocked to come across a yard full of children, most of whom were in beds or wheelchairs.

These are children no one wants. They are the blind, the crippled, the mentally or physically handicapped, but at this place, every child is treated with loving kindness by Gladys and her staff, who mother them in place of their absent parents. Gladys and her workers believe and live the Psalm "children too are a gift from the Lord;" (Psalm 127:3)

The home is one of the few in Haiti that specializes in caring for the mentally or physically handicapped.

Some of the children are found abandoned outside medical facilities; Gladys calls them her "gifts;" The pressure of caring for her helpless charges is enormous. Sometimes she is so overwhelmed she cries, but she keeps going forward because her kids need her.

"I feel like I'm doing something for God; It's a mission for me," she said; "You have to do it with your heart;" The work isn't a mere job, but a calling from the Lord. Wow, I thought, those words are so powerful! I had felt a calling myself towards this sort of work since my first visit to Jamaica back in February of 2006. I had since prayed about it, wondering how and where to begin; Gladys' words and heart, as well as the whole place really touched my very soul.

Because some of the children were abandoned and couldn't speak (meaning little information such as birthdays, is available), everyone's birthday is celebrated on Valentine's Day; It's one of the special touches that make Little Children of Jesus feel like a real home for the children.

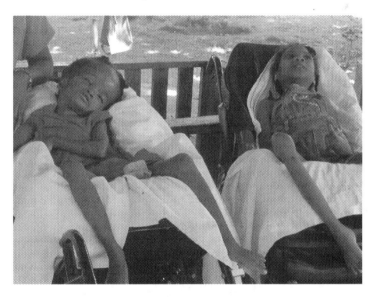

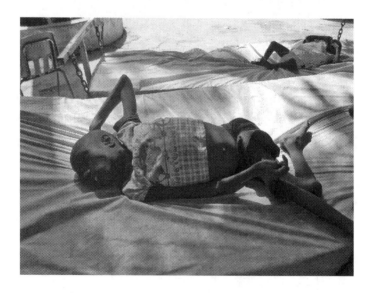

At the time of my visit there were 101 children there. I have no idea how the staff takes care of them all so well but they must love the children tremendously. They are constantly ministering to one somewhere and have little time to just "be with them"; so for the kids to see a bunch of people come in to visit and just spend time with them is a real treat.

Feeling overwhelmed with so many kids and not knowing which direction to walk, I usually go the opposite direction from the group wanting to make sure everyone gets some attention. Many of the children are very profoundly handicapped and there is little response if any. But sometimes you can see in their eyes how happy they are to have you with them.

As I walked around wheelchairs and between beds, trying to savor every second, I thought about the kids, what were they thinking? What did they want from me, a visitor? What could I give them? A smile or maybe hold a hand, a little peck on the cheek and a hug? So many kids I thought. So much need everywhere. I was in the middle of 100 children needing love. And as we walked through trying to make eye contact with them all and sharing a smile, some would reach out wanting us in some fashion. I had a couple of kids who could walk follow me just wanting to be with me because I had knelt down and given them a hug and friendly hello and smile, not that they knew what I was saying because they don't speak English.

I walked over to a group of beds and I saw a little girl smiling broadly at me. I found out later her name was Dora. I sat on the bed next to her and she just smiled. I talked, telling her how beautiful she was and how

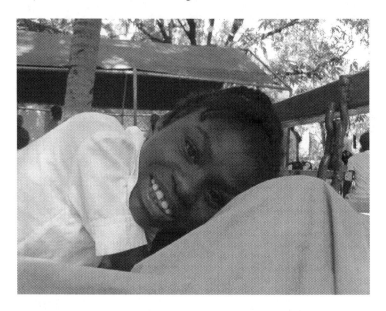

I loved her smile. She didn't say anything but just smiled and looked at me. I said, "I know I'm funny looking aren't I?" I made a silly laugh and she seemed to smile a little bigger. I figured I would head over to another bed as there were so many to see, so I leaned over to give her a kiss and then she did it. She giggled and started to laugh. I sat back up and I said, are you ticklish? I bent forward to kiss her again on her head and she laughed some more and then I laughed with her.

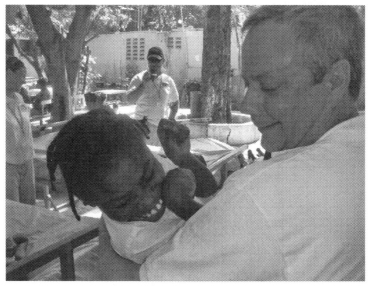

Dora couldn't talk, she couldn't even move. Her body was severely contorted and all she could do was lay there, but boy could she smile and laugh. I immediately fell in love with her. She had the most amazing and infectious laugh and she lifted my spirits so much with that universal language of laughter. I asked one of the staff members if I could hold her and I was told yes, so I said, you wanna go for a walk Dora? I know she couldn't comprehend my words, but looking into her eyes, I felt like she almost understood. I put my arms under her and lifted her up; I had worked a summer during school with Heritage Christian Services and was pretty comfortable around people with disabilities and had some experience with handicapped children. I was watching her closely to make sure I wasn't scaring her or worse yet, causing her pain; I lifted slowly and as I watched her eyes, they grew big and bright and she began to laugh and smile the biggest smile I have ever seen.

She weighed about 60lbs at most, but she felt like a feather in my arms. I began to walk around with her showing her the other children. I wanted them all to see her smile, and hear her laugh because it was so beautiful.

I started to sing silly songs and pretended we were dancing, swaying back and forth, doing little turns. We both smiled and laughed together the whole time. I was lost in the moment until I noticed a group of the children were watching us, all smiling and laughing, some hysterically. Apparently Dora and I had become quite the entertaining duo. I had found a way to connect with a group of kids all at once. I went to put Dora down back in her bed and we shared a smile again and another kiss on the cheek.

As I stood, a young girl tugged at my shirt, she must have been about 7 years old, and she pulled my arm to another young boy in a bed, much like Dora. There was no staff member around to ask what his name was so I never knew. He looked up at me and I knew the girl, maybe his sister, wanted me to give that little boy a ride like I had done with Dora. So I reached down and picked him up.

I walked around with him and showed him off to all my new friends. He had a great smile also and a little giggle that just rolled out from his belly. A little girl in a wheelchair waved frantically for my attention so I sat next to her with my friend. I made some silly noises like you would do with a baby and all three of us just laughed. I was having the time of my life. I had forgotten about the hurts and difficulties of Haiti for a while, and specifically the sufferings of the children. Instead we were all just

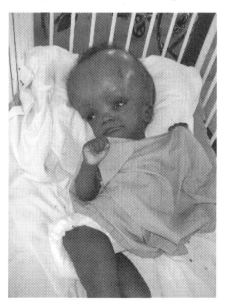

enjoying the moment and having fun. I LOVED it there! I can't express in words how quickly and how much I fell in love with those kids, and how much love I felt back—all in a matter of minutes. These were kids that a parent didn't want or could not take care of. They would live out their days in these conditions due to no medical support other than that what was available to address the most basic needs of survival. Some of these children had lost an opportunity at a normal, healthy life simply because their mothers had not received proper medical support and nutrition while pregnant. There were at least five children there suffering from Hydrocephalus, or "water on the brain". It can develop simply because the mother did not have enough to eat in her first trimester in some cases, which is common here. These were always the toughest on me since meeting Angel back in Jamacia. They always reminded me of her and I would never forget her face and how God spoke to me through her. I missed her but knew she was in a far better place now and for that I was happy.

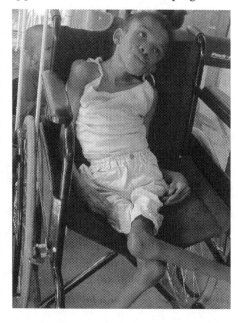

Each of these children have stories. They all have some form of handicap, and they are all the little children of Jesus. I went there thinking I was the one doing the giving, but as I left and said my tearful goodbyes, it was the children who were giving to me. Sometimes we walk into a situation not sure what will happen. I was filled with worry and fear not knowing what to do or say. But when I left, I was filled with

happiness and love, I had said very little because the children couldn't talk, but we could share smiles and laughs—and that was all I needed. I simply had to love and put my trust in God to get me through.

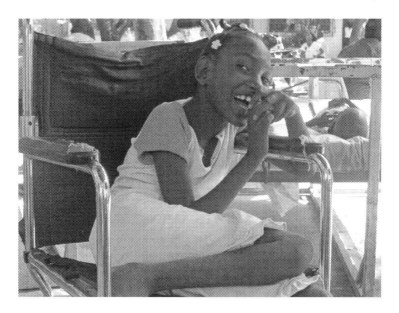

As I boarded the bus I was sad—not for the kids, that I had to leave. It was like being in heaven for me, so much joy and love. Gladys' mission was to stay with them and love them. I just wanted to stay with them too, but I had to come back and do my mission work, what God was calling me to, and that's to share their story with you. In the midst of the worst poverty and misery you can imagine, (you can't imagine unless you've been here and stood in it,) you can always find a piece of heaven. What came out of this experience was one of the most beautiful and loving experiences of my life. Gladys knew her mission in life—and now I was beginning to see more clearly what mine was as well, to help our brothers and sisters in developing countries. Maybe I could bring some happiness into the midst of something terrible.

NICARAGUA

I don't know if I have ever been in a place where I was more overwhelmed with the sheer beauty of the landscape than Nicaragua. It is known as the land of volcanoes and lakes. While Haiti is far and away the poorest place in the Western Hemisphere, Nicaragua, Ecuador and Honduras in Latin America rotate as the second, third, and fourth poorest.

I spent about ten days in Nicaragua in May of 2010 with Catholic Relief Services. It was a wonderful trip. We spent time driving throughout the country in a small bus, stopping to meet different people and learning about all the facets of their lives. The people are wonderful and always dressed in their Sunday best to meet us, like we were special or something. Despite how poor they may have been, we were always offered a meal and invited into their homes as honored guests. It was humbling to be treated so graciously.

I was told to expect this treatment as it is part of their culture, but also because we symbolize hope to the people. It is a very rare event that people from the United States come into their homes and listen. Listen to their history through civil war, dictatorship, abusive government, and crime. To hear how they struggle to survive and the difficulties they face each and every day of their lives.

I want to share a little bit about two different groups of people I met while here. I think they might best demonstrate the spirit that lies within them to succeed and create a better future for themselves.

Fundacion Entre Mujeres (Foundation for Women) was established fifteen years ago and now operates in fourteen countries teaching empowerment strategies for women. Perhaps unusual to many in the United States, women are still viewed as lower class citizens in much of the world. These situations are created from oppression and repression, social conduct, and culture. This organization teaches women about their rights and tries to build them up during difficult situations which happen frequently. Fundacion Entre Mujeres offers micro financing, loans of $500 and guidance, education and basically a helping hand.

The first thing they do is provide women access to land, the most valuable of resources in developing countries. Thus far the Foundation has garned 200 manzanas within Nicaragua, which equates to about 345 acres of land. They broke the land into eighty farms throughout the country.

I was able to meet a group of eight women who owned a seven—acre farm growing coffee in the mountains. Often times the land the Fundacion is able to obtain is not the best, but it's something, and in the mountainous country of Nicaragua, coffee is a crop that grows well due to cooler mountain temperatures. The older the plant, the better the coffee bean—but, the less beans it produces. That often puts farmers in a quandry, trying to decide between more coffee beans or better coffee beans.

In a male dominated country and culture where woman are clearly considered second class citizens, the women I met have overcome to achieve and break away from terrible situations in their own lives. To hear their stories is difficult, filled with repression and violence, most often from their husbands. Many men feel the woman is only meant to serve and do what they're told. While the country reports unemployment at approximately 8%, in 2008 before the country revised their formula to calculate unemployment, the rate was 22%. In addition, I learned from those I met that underemployment was closer to 45%-50%.

This group of women we met had overcome much in their personal lives, some divorced due to husbands that would not support them. However they are driven to succeed and obtain a better life not only for themselves, but for their children, family and community. The women had taken their small piece of land and developed ten mini-projects, such as their own organic fertilizer business, and built cabins in the field and promote agro-tourism.

The opportunities the women I met have taken advantage of have allowed them to participate in Fair Trade coffee programs that you may be familiar with and purchased from. Fair Trade is the business of paying people fairly for their work and efforts. With so many people in severe poverty Fair Trade can be part of a solution. Fair trade products such as coffee, not only increase family incomes, but also allow communities to invest in infrastructure such as sanitation facilities and health clinics. It also allows families to send their children to school

Up until the end of my trip, when I arrived in Managua, I had spent most of my time in the mountains. I spent my time mostly meeting farmers and coffee growers. In the big city though, there was no land to grow anything. I knew I was in for an experience as we left the heart of the city and traveled into a very poor section. There were literally 50 if

not more police waiting for us when we finally exited the bus. We were at the Monsignor Oscar A. Romero Center, a walled-in facility with barbed wire on top of ten foot walls. It was painted brightly with beautiful artwork on the outside that spoke of peace, love, hard work, hope and opportunity, various positive messages.

We walked in and were greeted by at least 100 children of all ages, from eight to twenty I would guess. My Spanish was not very good but I was able to talk to some of the children. We entered a large room full of kids and young adults who sat around the room on the floor. Of course we were given the chairs as we were honored guests. As I looked at them, all I could think was how young their faces looked.

Then some of them began to stand up and tell us their stories. The center itself stood on what used to be a vacant lot where the locals would dump their trash. Sister Nancy, a nun from Minnesota, had come to Nicaragua about ten years before my visit on a missionary trip and never left. She decided to stay in the burrios after meeting some of the children, hearing their stories, and seeing the dire need as those who felt they had no future or hope. The Children told us they felt their only hope of survival was to join a gang. Many came from families who could no longer take care of them. There was not enough food, clothing, medicine. Most had little education and felt they had no future. Instead they turn to survival mood, just trying to survive each day.

They join gangs because gangs allow them to feel part of something, like a new family. They get what they need to survive another day. As the gangs takes care of their own. The leaders take what they need and ensure those in the gang have what is needed or desired. But there is a cost of selling yourself to a gang. You do what you're told. After the children are accepted into the gang, they soon learn they've become part of a very violent world. They see their friends killed, they live by taking from those in society who are weaker, eventually feel trapped and don't know how to get out. I was told by one young man that he stole from his mother because the gang was his new family.

Sr. Nancy saw all this firsthand but instead of worrying about her own safety, she worried about those in the community. She gained the respect of the community after some time. They, including the gangs, realized she was only there to offer support and she loved all unconditionally. It didn't matter what you had done in your past, what mattered was today and your tomorrow. "Where can we go from here?" was her constant question. How can we make today and tomorrow better?

She eventually gained enough support from within the community just by being with them and loving them. Especially the kids, who want so desperately to have a future filled with hope and the possibility of a positive outcome in their lives. So the kids and Sr. Nancy started to answer the question she always asked and started to build a place for the kids within the community. Together they built the actual building we were standing in today, about seven years ago. Sr. Nancy had received some donations from her fellow Sisters in Minnesota to buy materials, then they worked at cleaning the lot and building the facility. A couple of friends and other volunteers flew down to teach the kids the trades of masonry, electrician, plumbing, and various construction of all types.

They all took great pride in their work and it is now looked upon as a safe zone within this community. The gangs stay away, and the young kids or adults now come here to learn various trades or vocations that they can use to better their own personal situations. The people of this community now have hope and a future filled with promise.

As we sat there, about six or seven young people stood up, each telling their individual story of how they now had hope and what this place had done for them. They learned various trade such as cosmetology, how to

55

run their own businesses. It filled them with great pride that they were able to break away from the gangs and help their families.

After listening to the kids tell us about overcoming their situation we were later given a tour of the neighborhood itself. That is why there were so many police around in the pictures you see. We were accompanied by dozens of police whereever we went because it is so dangerous there. The crime and gang warfare are extreme. It is literally a warzone some days as one policeman put it. People die here every day, all just trying to survive, how ironic. A large police presence was necessary the day we were there to ensure our safety and make sure we weren't kidnapped or robbed. Americans apparently bring a lot of money making them targets of crime. Sr. Nancy survives because she had committed herself to the people and is willing to die for them. She tells them that if they kidnap her, there will be no money coming, that she is worthless to them, and she is prepared to die with and for the people she has come to love as her own.

Like the name on the facility, Oscar A. Romero, I would consider Sr. Nancy a modern day saint, not worried about her own life, but about those she serves. She doesn't judge anyone, but loves them regardless. She fights for the innocent and gives everything she has to help others. In this burrio where hell is all around, Sr. Nancy brings that ray of light and hope and the gift of a future filled with life. She has literally saved hundreds of lives through her gift of love. By just caring, offering hope, love, and her tremendous faith in God, she is making a difference one life at a time. Where ten years ago was a lifeless lot filled with refuse, now comes the most beautiful light and precious gifts of all, a future for many filled with hope and promise.

"I NEVER LOSE HOPE"

It was an exciting time for me. After years of trying to raise money on my own, I finally had the idea to reach out to some friends at a college reunion. I had spent years raising money to build a tilapia farm in Haiti, but it was slow, slower than I was comfortable with. So I asked some friends for help, and I was blessed to find six that would. What resulted was a group called Eight 4 Third World Hope, later shortened to Eight 4 World Hope. There were eight of us in the group, Jesus being number one, then myself and my six friends. The "Eight 4" also signified that we had all graduated from St. John Fisher College in 1984.

I had worked with Food for the Poor (FFP) for years now and they were the perfect fit for my idea. Using their expertise and knowledge, we would partner with them on various projects, specific ones that our group would target to raise funds for and build. Our first project was a Basic School in Concord, Jamaica. I was adamant that we would do things a little differently with our group than traditional charitable organizations. I was always a little troubled when donating to a cause because I always wondered just where exactly did the money go? I saw the good work being done and they are always wonderful and very needy causes, but if I was going to make myself uncomfortable by asking others for money, I wanted to be able to show and tell them exactly where each dollar went.

So in January of 2011, I, along with my daughter Allison, who I brought to keep me company, flew to Jamaica to see firsthand the need. I wanted to make sure it was real, that the people were real, and that the community in fact needed this school. We were greeted by Susan James, project coordinator in Jamaica for FFP and Sheldon, who was in charge of FFP construction projects on the island.

We set out for Concord the next morning, which turned out to be a two-hour drive from Kingston. Up and down hills, sharp curves left and right, it was a real roller coaster ride. It reminded me of the first time I had come to Jamaica and had visited a village in what seemed the middle of nowhere. How did they find these people? In this case, the principal had written a note to FFP pleading for help as the Jamaican school authority was going to close down their school due to unsafe conditions. It took a week for the letter to be delivered because they were so remote.

Eventually when we arrived, we met the teachers, the children and Mr. Smith, the custodian. We received a tour of the school, which was really just a big room in the back of a church. It was very cramped for 30 kids! You could see water damage in the ceiling that leaked badly and the building was infested with bats. The main concern was the mold that was growing within the structure which caused respiratory issues for the children. The principal explained how she had dedicated her life to this school and how badly the children needed an education to enter primary school. Education is the key to everything there . . . to get a good job,

to escape poverty, to be able to live and survive. After a short time, I was convinced that this was indeed a very worthy project and I could go back home and look people in the eyes and say "please help." I saw the need and I knew I would come back to make sure the project was accomplished, and show donors exactly how their dollars touched the lives of so many.

We got back into the car and started to head back to Kingston. I was feeling good about everything. We were going to build a school that would serve hundreds of children over the coming years. We would live up to that word "Hope," in our name. The principal thanked us for visiting and helping, renewing their own hope that they would still have a school the following year. I was excited and couldn't wait to get back home and start raising money for such a great need.

As we hit the road Allison and I wondered about the next level of schooling, the primary school. Where would "our" kids go after basic school? About four or five miles down the road was a school up on a hill called Bensonton Primary School. Sheldon mentioned he had stopped by a couple years ago and they had asked for help, but there were no funds

available at the time. Susan said she is constantly being asked to "come see our need" all over Jamaica, but since they were out this way, maybe we could stop by and at least let them know we haven't forgotten about them. Allison and I jumped at the opportunity to see some more of Jamaica and see where our kids were headed after basic school. So we turned around and went back up the hill and pulled in. Getting out of the car we were greeted by the school guidance counselor. He recognized Sheldon and was happy to see us.

Mr. Omar Brady grew up in Bensonton and had gone off to Canada for a college education and work. He returned five years ago, wanting to help the community he grew up in, and specifically the school he attended as a young boy. He was very committed to making sure the children in Bensonton received a quality education and an opportunity with which he had been blessed.

He introduced us to the principal, Mrs. Coke, and we were given a tour of the school. Again, it was very cramped, over 170 kids packed into spaces that were far too small, but they made do with what they had. We explained that we were going to try and raise money to build a new school just down the road in Concord. He was pleased to hear that as he knew the Ministry of Education had ordered it closed for unsafe conditions, and said that the kids really did need that education before coming here.

He said, "luckily, we passed," (the government inspection) but he told us they needed to get much work done. Looking around, I could see that was pretty obvious. Walls were starting to bow out and there were water stains in the ceiling panels. Frankly I was surprised that it passed an inspection. Many things jumped out at me, but especially the need for better sanitation. He proceeded to walk us around back to a couple of pit latrines. Just getting within 30 yards of them made you want to turn around and run. The smell was awful and there were bugs, small lizards and flies all around. As I saw a few young kids walk in and out, you could see the disgust on their young faces.

Mr. Brady told us the latrines were about 40 years old and in great disrepair. It was so bad that the children were scared to use them. In fact, a small child had fallen into a pit at another school just nine months earlier. Word had gotten out and now the children were developing urinary tract infections, bladder infections and kidney problems from not going to the bathroom. Some children were actually leaving school early to go home and not getting the education they so desperately needed. They were scared to go in the pit latrine.

Sheldon asked if he was getting help to fix or replace them. Mr. Brady went on to tell us how about two and a half years ago, some people came from a church and he told them of the great need. He hadn't heard back from them but he hasn't lost hope. "At least they know how bad our need is and now you do also," he said, "I never lose hope".

The children were starting to get out of school for the day and we spent about 30 minutes talking and taking pictures. The school at one point had over 250 kids but it was now closer to 175. It was already packed. I wondered where they put the other 75 when they were here. I asked some of the kids about the bathrooms and it was quite the joke with them . . . well at least with the boys. The girls were just more disgusted. We said our goodbyes and headed back to our hotel in Kingston. Having Susan and Sheldon with us was invaluable. They had seen so much throughout the island and they knew what was in dire need versus what could wait. We threw some numbers around and Allison and I went away feeling like we had to try and help, but how were we going to ask people for money for toilets?

I started to laugh about all the possible bathroom jokes, but in my heart I felt we had stumbled across our second project. Now the question was . . . could I convince the group to go along with me? Building a school sounds great and everyone knows the value of an education, but building toilets seemed like an even bigger challenge to me. God had brought me this far so all I could do was place it in His hands and see what happened.

On the drive back and subsequent plane ride home, I saw a transformation take place in front of my eyes. It was Allison. While I had this life-changing experience years ago, she seemed to be going through it now. I always tell people . . . it is one thing to see pictures or hear stories, but to be in the middle of it is an experience you can't convey, you just live it. I know working in developing countries is not for everyone, but Allison was now fired up. She was filled with passion to help and was adamant about helping Bensonton school with the sanitation project. While I am a quiet and reserved person, she is very outgoing and not at all shy. She talked all the way back to the hotel, in the room, at the airport, and on the flight home. Yes, my heart was burning to help and now her heart was as well. It was nice to have someone else who understood as much as I did since only one of the other board members had ever been to a developing country. We later met with the group to share our experiences and Allison did most of the talking, of course. Her passion easily convinced the group and we unanimously agreed that the Bensonton sanitation project had to be our second project. I remember driving home that night thinking how did we go from building schools to building toilets? But I knew in my heart it was the right thing to do.

It wasn't the easiest thing to market but the need was great. About nine months later, we had raised about $35,000, enough to build both projects. Allison, Matt Shue, Rod Christian and I (members of Eight 4 World Hope), and some donors and volunteers visited Jamaica in February 2012 to see the completed projects and be part of the dedication ceremonies. To hear the words of thanks and see the gratitude expressed was a real blessing. We had just built a school and ensured that the community of Concord could continue to educate their young children to give them a better future. People from all over the region came to the ceremony. This was a really big deal. There were some speeches and then they presented us with a plaque of appreciation. The whole event was wonderful and we left feeling great and excited seeing the end result of all our work, and knew we had done something special.

It was time to go to the second dedication of the day, the sanitation project at the Bensonton Primary School. I was looking forward to it as well since this one had been so much fun. I must admit, I thought it would be a much smaller production, since it was "just toilets" and not a whole new school.

Once we arrived and got off the bus, I immediately headed over to where the old pit latrines had been. I was thrilled to see the new facility. It was so nice, much better than I had pictured in my mind. The old ones had been replaced with a new clean building that had flushable toilets, sinks and a septic system.

I gave Allison a hug and said this is so great! You had a big role in this happening and thanked her. The others in the group started to walk around to check things out when we were asked to go into the church for a ceremony and dedication.

We walked in and most of the church was already filled with students, parents, teachers, and various others. I was a little surprised at the number of people and I started to get nervous because I knew I would have to stand up in front of them to say a few words. The ceremony started and speakers began to talk, thanking the construction workers, FFP, and our group. Then the kids performed a song and dance for us called: "Bad Things Happen in a Pit Latrine!" It was geat and I truly enjoyed watching them. They even enacted a child falling through one of the old latrines, so you knew it had been on their minds.

Then the principal, Mrs. Coke, stood up to talk and it was there that I started to realize just how big a deal this was to them. I guess, even to this point, it was just toilets as far as I was concerned. I knew it was a nice addition to the school and it was now a safe and clean environment for the children, but that all changed as she began to speak.

She spoke of how she prayed for this day. How she was fearful for the children and staff having to use the pit latrines. How she loved her staff and all of the children in this school, both past and present, that she loved them all like a mother loves her child. Tears began to well up in her eyes as she spoke. She said "I have prayed for this day for 25 years now, I never gave up knowing God listened to our prayers. I never lost hope and I knew someday God would answer my prayers. Today is the day my prayers have been answered. I can now retire knowing this terrible thing has been replaced by this gift from God. I want to thank God for this miracle, for sending us Food for the Poor and Eight 4 Third World Hope."

I was stunned to hear such words, that this project for which we had raised money in about six months was something for which this woman had prayed 25 years. That she considered it a miracle. That she would actually shed tears over something I just took for granted, something I never much thought about.

We all went outside for the ribbon-cutting ceremony. As we gathered around the new building, one of the teachers gave an opening prayer which touched my heart, driving home how grateful the people were. It was so heartfelt, so filled with gratefulness, so profound that I was ashamed I hadn't realized just how much this meant to the people there. Her prayer went on for at least ten minutes in the hot sun of Jamaica, but I didn't mind.

I realized just how much more I had yet to learn about my mission here in the developing world. It became clear that I was still sometimes lacking in my own understanding of the needs that we were trying to meet. I thought about all of the other things in life I take for granted, the things that are always there when I need or want them and how I don't even give these things a second thought. Meanwhile, something as simple as a toilet is the answer to a prayer and considered a miracle in someone else's life. I never thought I would sustain a man's hope that we might build toilets at a school. I never dreamt that I could be involved in a ceremony and dedication of toilets, actually answering people's prayers.

A year earlier we just happened to stop by, wanting to see where "our" kids from the basic school would be headed next. Was it a miracle we just stopped in? I tend to think maybe it was the first member of our group, God, taking us by the hand and directing us there, giving hope to the community by our presence, answering the prayers of many by raising the money, and allowing all of us to be part of a miracle.

JOHN

It was our last day in Jamaica 2012 and we were off to pay a visit to Golden Acres, a community for people with severe disabilities. I had been there a couple times previously and I wanted to take the group I brought down for the dedication of our first two projects to visit this special place. Part of my goal was to give the group a look at some of the other services and good works being done in Jamaica.

I came to Jamaica in 2006 on my first trip and I really loved the people. One of the people who really touched my heart back then was a man named John. He had the biggest smile and he was so thrilled to have company. I remember walking into his room, where four others also lived, and immediately being greeted by that huge smile of his.

John couldn't talk but that smile was all he needed as far as I was concerned. The rest of his body was emaciated from years of being malnourished, his arms and legs nothing more than skin and bones.

He was laying on the floor when I entered. As I surveyed the room, the others were in beds all looking at me and seemingly excited that I was there. I took a picture of one woman and showed her the picture on my camera, she smiled broadly and was happy to see herself. As I did this, I felt my leg being grabbed, I looked down a little startled and saw it was John as he looked up smiling.

I knelt down on the floor and he continued to reach for me, so I laid down on the floor and put my arm around him. I had someone in my group take a picture of us and then showed him. As I sat there I noticed his leg was tied by the ankle, to his bed. When a staff person came by, I asked about it and she told me how John often tried to crawl off seeking someone to be with. Sometimes we can't find him or he gets too close to someone who might hurt him. He desperately wants to be with someone all the time.

I looked back at him and he was just laying there smiling at me and holding onto my arm as well as he could. In my mind I flashed back to a time when I was in college. I went to Kentucky on a mission trip with Glenmary and I was at a nursing home. The group of us were each assigned a person to whom to take lunch. My room had a man who was around forty who had suffered a stroke. As I sat down with him to chat, he noticed my shirt which had my school logo on it, St. John Fisher College. "What the hell is that on your shirt" he asked, and I told him it's where I go to school. He then said, "you aint Catholic or something are you?" I smiled and said yes, thinking this might be an interesting conversation. To my surprise he yelled at me to get the hell out of his room. I was shocked as he continued to tell me "get out, GET OUT. Go to Hell!"

After a few more anti-Catholic expressions I left him and was standing in the hall wondering what to do next? All of the other guys on our trip were with people and I was honestly a little shaken, I had never experienced someone hating me because of my faith.

I started walking slowly towards the lobby and I passed a room with a woman moaning and crying. She was looking out the door at me. I looked down the hallway but nobody was around so I went in to see what was wrong. Maybe there was something I could do to help without bothering one of the nurses. As I entered she reached for my hand, latched on to it and immediately settled down. She held my hand tight like she was afraid to fall, even though she was lying in a bed. I stood there for a few seconds trying to figure out what was wrong, but she seemed fine. So I said you're ok, I will tell the nurse to come see you, and I tried to walk away. As soon as our hands separated, she began to panic again and started to yell to me. I grabbed her hand and again, she calmed right down.

I sat with her the rest of the hour, just holding her hand. She was peaceful and calm the whole time. I couldn't help but think about how God had showed me how I could be hated so much by one person, and then so appreciated by someone else all in the matter of minutes.

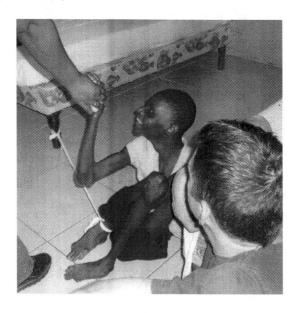

Now John was here, 25 years later in my life, just thankful for my presence. And as I sat with him, I started to think about how much I appreciated his presence also. That first visit to Jamaica had been too much for me. The pain and suffering, the way I saw people being forced to live, the battle just to survive each day, it was overwhelming. I was numb from all the hurt and the emotional rollercoaster I had been on. Just sitting there with John made me feel good. I think I needed him more than he needed me.

Like the lady in Kentucky, John wanted me to be with him, nothing more. We sat together as long as they let me, then we said our goodbyes. He was immediately someone special to me because I could feel God loving me through him. God must have known how much I was the one in need during my first visit and He was there through John, reaching out and holding me as well as he could. He was showing me I was loved and thanking me for coming to Jamaica, listening to His call to be with His children, our brothers and sisters.

Perhaps John needed me, but as I left I realized that I was the one who needed his smile and friendship which couldn't have come at a better time. He reminded me that I need to be ministered to also, and that God will be there when I need Him, even if I don't realize it at the time.

As I walked back to the bus, after meeting John for the first time, a little girl came up to me, she had Downs Syndrome and she had a great smile. I knelt down to say hello and she jumped into my arms and hugged me tightly. She surprised me but I truly enjoyed the hug. We took a picture together as I left with John and the little girl in my heart, thanking God for caring and loving me along this difficult journey.

I was really mentally and emotionally exhausted from all that I had seen the previous days.

Five years later I was on the way back to Golden Acres, and I was going to see John. I was so excited. It had again been a difficult trip seeing all the poverty, hurt, and need, but it was also filled with great joy at the new friends, the opening of our first school and sanitation project. I included this part of the trip into our itinerary to provide everyone with a broader view of the need, as well as to allow me to see my buddy John. Leaving Jamaica was always best after having the chance to be with John and feel his love and share in his happiness.

As we neared, I mentioned to one of the guides that I was anxious to see John and how much he meant to me. It was then that I was told that John died, about six months earlier from pneumonia. My heart sank, my hopes and excitement vanished with the shock of the news.

I thought to myself as tears welled up in my eyes how much I needed John. God I asked, why did you take him from me? I looked out the window as our bus drove on, getting ever closer. I was so filled with mixed emotions, happy for John that he was rid of his earthly body, and that he now was with God, freely moving, in the presence of our creator. I was so happy for him, yet I was so sad for myself, to the point of being angry because I was so selfish, wanting him here with me. I was grieving for my friend and in ten minutes I had to get off the bus and put on a happy face. I remember how I wanted to see him so badly, but he was gone.

The bus pulled in and everyone started to get off, I had trouble doing that. I was the last one off, not knowing if I could hide my tears from the group. I prayed to myself that the Lord would get through this part of the trip. How would I walk into John's room and not see him? Damn, I needed him, his smile, and his holding me back! I needed to feel that love.

I was in full blown self pity mode. I just wanted to sit there and not get off the bus, but I knew I had to. I slowly stood up and took a deep breath and wiped my eyes one more time. The rest of the group was already walking toward the housing units when I stepped off the bus. I started to cross the street, dreading the thought of walking into John's room without seeing John. Then out of nowhere, I was practically tackled by the little girl I had met years ago. She hugged me around my legs and as soon as I realized it was her, I fell to my knees in the middle of the road and hugged her. We held each other tightly, for what seemed minutes. I stayed there with my faced buried into her shoulder, until a car honked its horn at us to move.

I started to cry as I hugged her, thanking God for sending her into my arms like this. I needed her so badly at that point, God knew it and I believe He sent her to me. I stood up and she grabbed my hand and led me to my group, walking together towards the housing units. All I could think of was how gracious God is to me, sending me this little girl to hug me when I needed it most. I then knew I would be ok, that God had just reminded me that I am not alone. He is with me every step of the way. God was this little girl, reassuring me, guiding me, and telling me to keep moving forward, that there is more to do.

I introduced my friend to the group and she passed out hugs to everyone. After visiting a few in the home, I headed to John's room. I wanted to see it, remember it, say a prayer for him while in it. I wanted to tell him how much he meant to me, that I loved him, and share how happy I was for him to be free of his withered earthly body, now free to soar like an eagle in heaven.

I walked into John's old room and there were four people in it. A new woman laid in the bed that used to be John's, her name was Faith. All I had to do was see that name tag and I lost it. I teared up, again. Ok God, I got it, you're taking care of him.

I looked down at Faith as she laid in her bed and smiled back up to me. She had a stuffed bear that she kept with her and it had fallen out of her reach. I picked it up and handed it to her and she smiled from ear to ear, so happy to have her teddy bear back. I thought about how sometimes it is the simplest of things that we do that can make others happy.

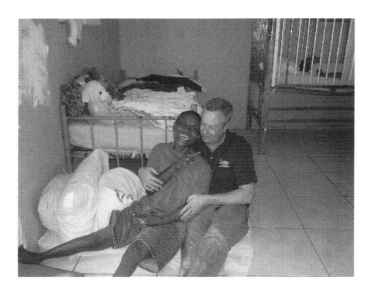

I looked across the rest of the room and there was a woman sitting on a pillow on the floor. Her name was Jasmine and she smiled and reached for me, calling for me as well as she could. I walked over and sat on the floor with her. I put my arms around her and she smiled. I sat holding on to her thinking about how I sat here holding my dear friend John many times before. I was grieving inside, but God was there with me through it all. I just sat with Jasmine, holding her and thinking about so many things. How happy I was for John, how much I missed him, and most of all, how so many people think we are the givers, building schools, providing food, housing or whatever, but the people here give back to in so many ways. Not with material things, but with their gifts of faith and love that some in the States don't seem to share as readily.

That day I saw God taking care of me through them. The little girl's hug, the woman named Faith, Jasmine, who like John, was on the floor just wanting someone to be with her. We all try to do what we can to help others, but this day, it was God ministering to me through them.

MCCOOK'S PEN—HIGH HOUSE BASIC SCHOOL

We had completed our first two projects with our group, Eight 4 World Hope, and had celebrated two dedications the day before. While still in Jamaica, we had more of an opportunity to visit potential projects, meet the people and community, and personally assess the need while developing a true understanding of the challenges so many in Jamaica face.

We went to a basic school called High House in McCook's Pen, St. Catherine. We drove up and down a couple of dirt side streets trying to locate it, and finally with the help of a few people in the community, we were able to track it down. I remember getting off the bus and thinking to myself, where is it? There was a beat up old shed to the left, a cemetery to the right with some abandoned old cars lying around. But upon taking things in a little more, I realized what I thought was just an old beaten shed was indeed the school.

I looked at the rest of the group, all of us a bit stunned with jaws dropped. That was it??? That was a school? But it was, the name of it was written in chalk on the outside wall of the building. As my mind tried to accept that this was indeed a school, we began to hear the children making noise inside, and people from nearby starting to come over to see us.

The dirt road had garbage and weeds all about and several dogs roamed freely. A small girl who was about five years old walked up to us with her mother. I said hello and introduced myself. I asked the little girl why she wasn't in school and she told me there was no room for her. Apparently there were about sixty children wanting to go to school but this school, if you want to call it that, could only hold forty at the most.

The school is owned and operated by the community and has been in operation since 1989. Its mission is to provide children 3-6 years old with a quality education mandated by the Ministry of Education (MOE), so that they are prepared to advance to the primary level.

I was told the school had some structural problems, but I had no idea it was as bad as it was. The pictures we took couldn't even do it justice. The main building was deteriorating, leaving large holes in the walls. The makeshift kitchen where they prepare meals for the children was made of old corrugated metal sheets that were barely staying together. It was so small that only one person could fit in it at a time. The bathroom was in a ghastly state. One toilet for all of the students and staff, essentially an old structure made of rotten wood that was, to put it nicely, clearly unsanitary.

The Early Childhood Commission (ECC) had required the school to renovate its facilities to be in full compliance with government regulations or face closing. As I talked with various parents I learned that if this school closes, they could not send their kids to school any longer due to the cost. The next closest school was several miles away and they would need to transport the kids via taxi back and forth. It was just too costly.

The Principal, Mrs. Roslyn Givens had been teaching at the school from its inception. She told us about the children she had taught over the years that had gone on to accomplish wonderful things. She was full of well deserved pride, but also the fear of losing the school. Somehow she had made this shack work for twenty some years, teaching the children of the community in the hopes of them having a better life. Many of the parents couldn't read or write and were desperate for their children to have that chance. Not having an education themselves they fully understood the value of being able to read and write.

As I walked around the building I found more graves behind the school. It turns out there was nowhere else to build, so they put the school in the entrance of a cemetery. To be honest I couldn't believe the place was even standing. Apparently, whenever it rained the teachers and students would gather in one corner that would remain somewhat dry. If it rained too hard, classes had to be cancelled because everything would get wet. It was hard to imagine how the teachers were able to teach at all in this environment.

The kids, of course, were the highlight for me. They were so happy and just loving life. We had brought school supplies that we shared with Mrs. Givens, but for the kids we brought candy and liquid bubbles. To see their faces light up is such a precious gift to me, they are always so happy. We took a lot of pictures and showed them to the children as they love to see themselves. After a few brief out of control moments, the kids gathered together to sing a few songs for us. We all behaved for a bit but then it was back to the free for all. Mrs. Givens had lost control of her kids, tough for any teacher, but I along with the rest of the group were having such a great time and wanted to play.

We settled down after about ten minutes and went into the school to do a bit of work. They showed us their reading and writing abilities and was quite surprised at how far they had progressed by age four or five. They were already learning to read and write; could all count to twenty and they knew their colors and alphabet. After a short time, we have to leave to go see other potential projects within Jamaica.

As I got on the bus I was thanking God that I had the group with me, to share this moment and to truly understand the need in Jamaica, the need of those who have no voice and nowhere to turn for help. The community is too poor and the government won't help. I tell our group that to see pictures and hear or read words is only part of it. I share that to have your other senses exposed and stand in the midst of the need that McCook's Pen really is, takes reality to another level. Even while writing this, I just can't describe it fully so you the reader could truly understand the need. I was thankful that three other board members, Matt, Rod and Allison were with me to share the experience.

We left knowing in our hearts that McCook's Pen would be our next project. When I received the proposal the following month I became a little worried as I learned, it would cost about $55,000 dollars. That was a lot of money for a group that just came together a year earlier. It was also $20,000 more than the other two projects combined, but in our hearts we knew we had to move forward. The need was so great and so we put our faith in God, our number one member, and began planning how to raise the funds.

Upon returning to the states, the group agreed we should apply for our 501c3 status, (tax exempt) so we could start to approach bigger donors. We continued with fundraisers that were built off the previous year, talked to groups such as Rotary, Kiwanis, church groups, and basically anyone who would listen. We also started to expand our horizons from Rochester and started to find others willing to help.

I could tell God's hand was guiding us as doors opened up out of nowhere. One of those doors is my friend Sonia Barton from Spring Valley, near New York City. She is from Jamaica and had felt a calling to help the primary school she attended back in Jamaica, which happened to be Bensonton Primary School. Upon calling the school, however, she found that we were already helping with new bathrooms. Wanting to help, she called me. I told her we had already raised the money for that project, our second, and told her about our group and McCook's Pen. She came to our next fundraiser and actually traveled back home to Jamaica to see for herself the school we were going to help next. That led to the Spring Valley Rotary donating $2,000 to the project and my meeting another member of the Rotary, Howard Goldin.

Howard and his friend Ed were former Vietnam soldiers, and returning to Vietnam one year, they saw the needs of the people and formed a group called S.T.E.P. (Schools To End Poverty). S.T.E.P. donated $4,000 to our McCook's Pen project. They have done tremendous work in Vietnam and Honduras, and I am proud to say in Jamaica now as well.

We also were contacted by a group in Rochester, New York that had heard about us and wanted to see if they could help. The Dorothea Haus Ross Foundation funds projects like ours around the world and they provided us with a grant of $10,000. It was just amazing, it was truly God guiding our efforts and by the end of 2012 we had most of the money so that we could break ground and start building at McCook's Pen.

I along with another group of people including my wife went back to Jamaica the first week of February, 2013 for the dedication of the school. The group were entirely different from the previous group so we stopped by to show them the old school. Much to my surprise one of the teachers as well as the kids were still there. They hadn't been in the new school yet, today would be their first day as well.

It had been a year since I had been back and there were a few new faces, but also some familiar ones, and the kids had different uniforms. This was a big day for the community and part of the celebration was new uniforms to go with the new school, a fresh new beginning.

At the old school, not much had changed from our previous visit, except the old stove they had before quit working and had been replaced by a propane tank hooked up to a little gas grill to cook for the kids. That was sometimes the only meal the kids ate all day, so it was essential they were somehow fed.

As we visited the kids I was able to focus on them and those I brought with me, since I has seen the building my earlier trip. I could see the disbelief in our group's eyes as they took the scene in. The school looked like an old broken down tool shed, another said "it is the size of my living room." The teacher who was there joked she would miss the occasional rat or lizard that came in during class through one of the many holes in the wall.

We took pictures of the kids and took one last look at what "was" the school before getting back on the bus to ride to the new school, about 300 yards away. The land had been donated by one of the local sugar companies and the company also donated some playground equipment and fencing. Eight 4 World Hope funded the rest.

I remember getting off the bus and thinking how much bigger the new school was. It was beyond what I expected and I just looked at it for a couple minutes as I tried to take it in. It was painted in yellow and blue and there were no holes in the walls or roof. I thought to myself that it was solid, sturdy, and safe, something that would last a long, long time. I think the first emotion I felt was one of accomplishment, which quickly turned to how blessed I was to be part of something so wonderful and joyous in so many people's lives in this Jamaican community.

The new school has three separate classrooms, computer room with six computers, sick bay, principal's office, dining area, flushable toilets and sinks with a septic system, and a kitchen with a new refrigerator and stove.

The principal, Mrs. Givens, was already at the school preparing for the dedication when we saw each other. We hugged each other as tears rolled down our cheeks. She kept saying thank you over and over, how beautiful it was, how her prayers had been answered, how the school meant so much to the kids and the community. I, on the other hand, had no words. I was overcome with it all. That moment was more than I had ever envisioned or dared to even dream when I asked my friends to help me raise money to help those in developing countries. It was an amazing thing, all of it, in so many ways. All I wanted to do was thank God for letting me be a small part of something so wonderful.

I knew that I would have to say a few words at the dedication representing Eight 4 World Hope but I was shocked to be handed a slip of paper that showed me as giving a keynote address. I was already searching for words, so overcome by all of it, now they expected a speech? All I could do was laugh and say I guess I'd come up with something. I wanted to sit with the group but I was seated at the head table with the chairman of Food for the Poor, the Mayor and top officials from the ECC and, of course, Mrs. Givens the principal. I felt totally out of place but what could I do? It was hot and we were thankfully all under a big tent. Reporters and news cameras were all rolling, parents and various dignitaries from Jamaica looked on.

When I did finally stand to talk, all I could do was let my heart take over. I told them I had nothing prepared and asked them to forgive me for that, and that all I could offer was what was in my heart. It went fine, as the people from Jamaica are always gracious. I told them that even though we are far away in America, they are always in our thoughts, hearts, and prayers. Instead of saying you're welcome, I told them I want to thank them for letting us be part of something so wonderful, for allowing us into their community and for being so welcoming. That God works in all of us and coming together, great things can happen. I believe God has great plans for all of us, each of us contributing in our own way to bless the children, each with the potential I shared to do great things.

I didn't know what to say, and still didn't as I wrote this three months later. It was such a big event it even made the front page of the Jamaican national newspaper. The new school was a gift from God in so many ways. A gift of a safe beautiful school for a community and a gift from God to me, reminding me how blessed I am with such a great family, friends and people who would give of themselves for others they never met.

I have since seen videos, articles, and stories about the school at McCook's Pen, but to me the effects will always be beyond any words I read or hear. I am filled with feelings and emotions of total gratitude to so many who helped and were a part of the efforts and my thank yous will never be enough.

IN CONCLUSION

1 Corinthians 12:4-7, 12-13
There are different kinds of spiritual gifts but the same Spirit;
there are different forms of service but the same Lord;
there are different workings but the same God
Who produces all of them in everyone.
To each individual the manifestation of the Spirit
is given for some benefit.
As a body is one though it has many parts,
And all the parts of the body, though many, are one body,
So also Christ.
For in one Spirit we were all baptized into one body,
Whether Jews or Greeks, slaves or free persons,
And we were all given to drink of one Spirit.

I hope you enjoyed these stories. I started writing this book as a way to share the stories of the people I've met, the people who often times have no voice. I have so many stories but these few will give you an idea of the reality in our world and the life so many of our brothers and sisters are forced to live. It's always hard for me to return from a trip to a developing country and assimilate back into our materialistic-based culture. In the Developing World it is not materialistic but rather about love of family and faith in God; so simple, and often times they're happier than we are with the gift of life.

Perhaps we have lost our focus on what is truly important in life and our many gifts. According to Catholic Relief Services, our country spends 1.12 trillion on our defense budget, and 100 billion on development and aid to help those in need. We could feed a family of four for a month for as little as $30, I wonder how much one missile costs us and how many we really need? While we are blessed to be able to plan for retirement, others plan on how to survive another week, how to feed their child or find a way to get medicine.

I know over the years it has been the teenager in the hospital, a small girl who could only move her eyes, orphans in Haiti, or a little girl hugging me when I was in need, taking my hand and showing me that everything would be ok. In each of them, I saw God and in each of them, it was God taking my hand walking this journey with me. God comes in all sizes, colors, faiths, peoples. God is all around and sometimes most vividly in those we don't want to be near.

This book was very difficult to write. It was mentally and emotionally draining as I relived the moments in detail. However it was also liberating and therapeutic to share them, rather than to just know and live with them in my heart each day. I had to find a way to tell their stories, to let people know how badly some people hurt. Thank you for giving me that chance.

As I look back at my initial fighting with God about my calling, in the end I realized that I am blessed and humbled that God would call me to this ministry. I just wish he would have revealed it to me sooner, but things happen in God's time, not ours. It is clear, though, as I look back, God was preparing me all along for this. If anything, I've learned so much about myself these past years and the learning hasn't stopped, nor will it ever. While we may have preconceived notions or see limits within ourselves, nothing is impossible to God if only we have faith and trust in Him.

I am thankful that God took my hand and led me, always teaching, supporting, and loving me. Like the scripture quote from Corinthians says, we all have gifts, each different and special. Eight for World Hope members each brought their parts, became one, and accomplished wonderful things, literally answering prayers and creating modern day miracles. The most exciting part of all of this is Sr. Nancy is right, knowing we can make today and tommorrow better. Where can we go from here? I am excited to see where God takes me next. I am already working on two more projects. A sanitation project for a school of 186 children ordered closed by the Ministry of Education due to the pit latrines being too dangerous for the children to use. Then a school in dire need of expansion for the 200 children who attend. It was also damaged badly by Hurricane Sandy.

Finally I hope you realize that you are invited to be a part of something wonderful somewhere in this world, whatever your gifts may be. Often times God held my hand and taught me through a child who couldn't move or talk, someone discarded or those seen as a burden by the world. For me, this is where I find God most. Keep an open heart, listen, see and allow God to work through you! Amazing things await!

God Bless you, Deacon. Kevin

Thank you!

MEDITATION ON HANDS

Think of the miracle that is your hand. Your hand—composed of many different parts. Think of your fingers. Each is a unique creation by itself. Move just your index finger. It seems to have a life of its own. It seems complete by itself. Yet this one finger cannot work unless it works in harmony with your other fingers. Complete by itself—and yet not complete.

Become aware of the air at your fingertips, between your fingers, on the palm of your hand. Experience the fullness, strength and maturity of your hands. Think of your hands—think of the most unforgettable hands you have held in yours—the hands of your father or mother, your grandparents, a spouse, friend or child. Remember the oldest hands that have rested in your hands. Think of the youngest hands you have held—your child's hands, your nephew or niece, or a tiny friend. Think of the incredible beauty, perfection, and delicacy in the hands of a child. Once upon a time your hands were that same size . . . .

Think of all that your hands have done since then. Almost all that you have learned has been through your hands—turning yourself over, crawling and walking while balancing yourself. Learning to hold something for the first time; feeding yourself, washing and dressing yourself. At one time your greatest accomplishment was tying your own shoes.

Think of all the learning your hands have done and how many activities they have mastered—the things they have made. Remember the first day you could write your own name?

Our hands have not been just for ourselves, but for others. How often they have been given to help another. Remember all the kinds of work they have done—the tiredness and aching they have known—the cold and the heat—the soreness and the bruises. Remember the tears they have wiped away, our owns or another's—the blood they have bled—the violence they have expressed—and think of how much gentleness, tenderness and love they have given.

Remember how often they have folded in prayer—a sign of both their powerlessness, and of their power. Our parents guided these hands in the great symbolic language of hands—the wave of a hand in "hello" or "goodbye", the handshake, the sign of the cross. Think of the number of times the beads of the rosary have slipped through these hands.

There is a mystery, which we discover, in the hand of a person whom we love. There is a special joy remembering the hand of the one we love—that special hand—which has given us what has been given to no one else.

But there are many other hands we cannot forget—the hands of a doctor, a nurse, an artist, a conductor, a teacher, or a friend. Think of the many hands that have shaped our lives.

Now—raise your right hand slowly and gently place it over your heart. Press more firmly until your hand picks up the beat of your heart, that most mysterious of all human sounds, your own heartbeat, a rhythm learned in the womb from the heartbeat of your mother. Press more firmly for a moment and then release your hand and hold it just a fraction from your clothing. Experience the warmth between your hand and your heart. Now lower your hand to your lap very carefully, as if it were carrying your heart. For it does. When you extend your hand to another, it is not just bone and skin, it is your heart. A handshake is the real heart transplant.

Think of all the hands that have left their imprint on you. Fingerprints and handprints are heartprints that can never be erased. The hand has its own memory. Think of all the places that carry your handprint and all the people who hear your heartprint. They are indelible and will last forever.

Now, without opening your eyes extend your hands on either side and find another hand. Do not simply hold that hand, but try to convey a message—friendship, concern. Let your hand speak and let it listen to the other. Try to express your gratitude for this hand stretched out to you in the dark. Now bring your hand back again to your lap. Experience the presence of that hand lingering upon your hand. The afterglow will fade but the print is there forever.

Whose hand was that? It could have been any hand; it could have been God's hand. It was. God has no other hands but ours. AMEN

Adapted from the book *Surprised by the Spirit* by Father

Edward Farrell.

ABOUT THE AUTHOR

With a BS in Economics from St. John Fisher College and a Masters degree from St. Bernard's School of Theology and Ministry, he was ordained to the Sacred Order of Deacons by His Excellency, the Most Reverend Matthew H. Clark, Bishop of Rochester NY in 2005. The father of four has been married for 23 years and run his own print business for the past 18 years in Canandaigua, NY. He has volunteered in many efforts to help others in his community his whole life. After a trip to Jamaica to see firsthand the need in a developing country 2006, he has since worked to spread awareness and raise funds to help those he has met as well as those who have no voice from all over the world. A Global Fellow with Catholic Relief Services and advocate for Food for the Poor, he travels to various communities to share his reality and tell of the good that has come from the tireless efforts of such groups. He founded his own group in 2010 called Eight 4 World Hope that focuses on specific projects, seeing the need before any funds are given, then returning to insure the funds have been applied properly to address the need. His goal is to hear the voice of those whose words all too often fall on deaf ears, then answer their prayers.

If you would like to help

www.Eight4WorldHope.org
or
Eight 4 World Hope
330 South Main St.
Canandaigua, NY 14424

Other organizations I encourage you to visit and support
(In alphabetical order)

Catholic Relief Services
www.crs.org

Dorothea Haus Ross Foundation
www.dhrossfoundation.org

Food for the Poor
www.foodforthepoor.org

JASY
www.JASY.info

Schools to End Poverty
www.schoolstoendpoverty.org